STEP-BY-STEP TO NATURAL FOOD

CANCER PREVENTION
through
THE WHOLISTIC WAY OF EATING

By
Diane Campbell

Illustrated by Mary E. Sandifer

CC Publishers
P.O. Box 4044
Clearwater, Fl.
33518

"I beseech you therefore, brethren, by the mercies of God, that ye present your bodies a living sacrifice, holy acceptable unto God, which is your reasonable service.

And be not conformed to this world: but be ye transformed by the renewing of your mind, that ye may prove what is that good, and acceptable, and perfect, will of God." *Romans 12:1 and 2*

To my wonderful family—*my husband, Robert, my daughters, Kayleen* and *Janeen* for all their encouragement

To my friend, *Rosalind Moore* — who introduced me to natural eating

STEP-BY-STEP TO NATURAL FOOD

Copyright © 1979 by Diane Campbell

1st Printing 10,000, March, 1979
2nd Printing 10,000, January, 1980

Library of Congress Catalog Card Number 79-84548

ISBN 0-9603766-0-7

Printed in the United States of America

CC Publishers, P.O. Box 4044, Clearwater, Fl. 33518

FOREWARD

Wholistic Healing—an idea whose time has come? Well no, not really. The philosphy has been around for centuries. The Bible speaks of it. Documents of ancient civilizations refer to it. Holistic healthful living is a broad term deserving our consideration. It's culmination in perfected body, mind and spirit produces a whole that is more than a whole, health as we *should* know it and experience it.

. . . And at the very basis, responsible nutrition. Diane has captured this need and has developed a very readable and understandable response in this book. Her goal, to help all people (and especially the cancer patient) eat better, is aptly expressed in this work. Her own story of her family's "conversion" to Holistic Living is beautiful to read and experience.

Natural foods, fresh and wholesome, simply and properly prepared are the stepping stones to good health, the building blocks of a responsible Holistic Health Program.

Now, dear Reader, mind your P's and Q's and all the other letters of the alphabet relating to vitamins and minerals, carefully study Diane's recommendations, do your nutritional homework and I expect to see you at graduation time at the head of your class in nutrition.

By Dr. Byron Goldberg

THE WHOLISTIC PROGRAM

The wholistic program is basically building the body's entire immunization system to fight disease. This is the key in cancer prevention. The wholistic approach to life consists of a natural diet, positive stress-free mental attitude, exercise, vitamin supplements and a spiritual relationship to God.

The best way to describe the diet explained in this book is to say — POISON FREE. It consists of all fresh vegetables and fruits, grains, sprouts, homemade breads, fruit juices, herb teas, seeds, nuts, cheese, yogurt, and goat's milk. Emphasis should be made on eating as many raw vegetables and fruits as possible. Meat protein is eliminated or kept to a very low part of the diet, using beans, cheese and nuts instead. Sugar, white flour and regular salt are not to be used. Honey, whole wheat flour and sea salt are used in their place. Pure drinking water, if there is any left on earth, should be sought after like gold.

As many people have said, "Everything is bad for us — there is hardly anything left on the earth that isn't polluted! Why don't we just give up?"

My answer is, "Don't give up, just keep checking yourself to get rid of all the harmful poisons you can. Each time you eliminate something harmful to your body, and replace it with something good; you have made progress. The harm comes when you know to do right and don't do it. The disaster comes when you allow your family to continue eating substances, mentioned in this book, which God never intended to go through our bodies."

TABLE OF CONTENTS

CHAPTER 12 *VITAMINS AND MINERALS* 170

WHY SHOULD YOU EAT NATURAL FOOD?

Have you ever wondered how our rugged ancestors, the pioneers, worked from dawn to dusk without aspirin or pep pills and yet survived tremendous odds? What was their secret? It was faith in the Lord and a wholesome, natural diet.

Americans are beginning to consider the pitfalls of convenience foods. No longer is our "hamburger" and "hotdog" image so beautiful. Every family is plagued by at least one cancer victim. It is not uncommon to know several people, at one time, dying of cancer. Even though the statistic is one out of four, if the real truth were known, one out of every three people will die of cancer. Heart disease is common among middle aged people. The average male over forty has one out of two chances of suffering from a heart attack before his sixty-fifth birthday. Strokes can strike a person even in his twenties.

We have known for years that certain foods aren't good for us, but we blindly eat our way through each day. Somehow, we rationalize that we have lived this long on bad food, "so what's another day!" The sad part of the 'blindness' to food is that we completely ignore what the Bible has to say about proper eating. In I Corinthians 6:19-20, we are taught, "What? Know ye not that your body is the temple of the Holy Spirit Who is in you, Whom ye have of God, and ye are not your own? For ye are bought with a price; therefore, glorify God in your body and in your spirit, which are God's."

How long can we ignore this Scripture telling us to take care of our bodies? God cares about our bodies and wants us to be healthy, not diseased. He instructed Adam in Genesis 1:29, "And God said, Behold, I have given you every herb bearing seed, which is upon the face of all the earth, and every tree, in which is the fruit of a tree yielding seed; to you it shall be for meat." In the beginning two thousand years plant food was man's diet; but God allowed him to add animal food in Genesis 9:2-3. And then meat was eaten only on festive occasions. But we have come so far from what God intended for us to eat. God instructed Adam to eat "every herb bearing seed." Somehow the rush of life in an overly sophisticated society has crowed out these jewels—the seeds—the beginning of life itself. There is the answer! Let's get back to eating natural foods: seeds, grains, nuts, vegetables, herbs and fruit. Let's throw off the bondage of disease and quit producing children that "catch" everything that comes along.

Even if you're not convinced to eat natural food, what about allowing your children or grandchildren to eat them? Don't they deserve the very best we can offer them? No parent would knowingly give poison to their children; and yet, every time you hand your child a soda pop or flavored drink, you are giving him chemicals that are stored in his body. Is it any wonder that twelve-year olds die of cancer, teenagers are afflicted with MS, and young men and women commit bizarre acts. We are killing ourselves with our food! The statistics say a person will eat approximately twenty-two pounds of chemicals in his food each year. That's a lot of poison.

HOW TO BEGIN

Now that you are interested in preserving your body, you will want to change to a better way of eating. If you are a drastic person, you may go into the kitchen, remove all your food, throw it out and start over. However, that doesn't go over too well with husbands. And so, you will notice a sensible, gradual, step-by-step program which changes the family without hurting anyone. Here is a list of helpful hints to get you started in the right direction.

HELPFUL HINTS

1. Don't take anything away from your family, until you replace the food with something better.
2. Don't change your favorite recipe to "natural ingredients" until you learn to cook and bake with them.
3. Do read every label of all food you purchase.
4. Do not buy anything with: Additives
Artificial coloring
Artificial flavoring
Preservatives
Sugar
Corn Syrup
Dextrose
Glucose
Brown Sugar
Raw Sugar
Turbinado Sugar
5. Don't get discouraged if you make something and no one likes it— try again with another recipe.
6. Do take time to make the change. Your family is worth the extra effort in the kitchen.
7. Don't be afraid to try new things. Your family may surprise you and like it.
8. Remember, eating is just a habit to Americans and you have to break the old habit and teach your family new principles of good eating.

9. Don't think about foods you used to eat. Concentrate on all the wonderful foods you will experience. Even try raw foods.
10. Don't make eating junk food a "sin" for your children. They should never be punished for eating the way you taught them. The only "sin" is when grown-ups know there is a better way to eat, and they don't do it. Instead of punishment, be an inspiration and a model for your children. Show them a better way.
11. Do be prepared to take your own food to church, social gatherings and parties. Always prepare extra special goodies for your children to take to parties. Don't expect them to sit and not eat.
12. Do buy all fresh vegetables and fruit. Stay away from cans and prepackaged foods. Buy frozen if you're desperate.

CHECK LISTS

You will notice at the end of each chapter a "check list." This list will be helpful for you to record the changes you are making. Changing the eating habits of your family will not be an easy job. It takes a lot of work and effort. Each member of the family must do his share. It must be a joint adventure. The father seems to be the key in getting this plan to work. When daddy says that he will try certain foods, then the children will try too. Children copy their parents. If they see you eating natural food and enjoying it, they will want to eat the same thing. What a boost when a daddy says, "Honey, this whole wheat cherry cobbler is delicious." What a struggle when a father comes home with a half gallon of surgary, chemical laden, benzyl-acetate ice cream, and tells you, "I just had to have some strawberry ice cream."

Keep a positive attitude toward natural food. Even when people persecute you, think about how much better your body will be. The old saying by Adelle Davis seems to catch up to us one day, "You are what you eat." Usually by then, it is too late to change. Remember, your eating pattern has been going on for years and it takes time to change old habits.

This book is an over all guide for people who wish to change their eating habits to a more natural way of life, with down-to-earth recipes. Every recipe in this book has been "people tested." You may start with any chapter. Just choose the area where you have the greatest need and don't forget to mark your check list. in this way, you can keep an accurate record of your progress.

MY STORY

At least three years before this book was written, I discovered that I had hypoglycemia or low blood sugar. It wasn't too hard to figure out, since I was continually tired. It was nothing for me to lie down three times a day and take a nap. Every morning I felt as though I had been run over by a Mack Truck. Of course, I accomplished absolutely nothing and was very discouraged with life. Also, I had a craving for sugar that wouldn't quit. There had to be something wrong with me, but no one seemed to know. Finally, a dear friend, Gladys Bruce got me in to see her doctor. With his knowledge of low blood sugar, the diet, and vitamins, I began to improve. My diet drastically changed the family's eating habits. After all, if sugar wasn't good for me, why should it be good for the rest of them? I moved through the kitchen like a tornado. Soon four bags of poison were carried out of my kitchen. I never dreamed so many things had sugar in them—everything from soup to soy sauce and crackers to canned corn. It looked like Mother Hubbard's cupboard *(ALL BARE.)* Slowly we started replenishing the shelves, picking and choosing what appeared to be better for us.

With the sudden interest in a new way of life, I began reading every health article in sight. It was a whole new world for us and it was very confusing. Then I realized that another friend, RosalindMoore had begun eating a natural diet without sugar, white flour, preservatives, colorings, additives, and packaged foods. It was during this time that we discovered that my husband had active cancer cells. After much prayer and seeing the wonderful results of others, we decided to use an alternative cancer therapy. Our diet now became even more important and we were so grateful for all the help the Moores gave us. My husband went on the Laetrile Program, with vitamins, enzymes and diet. Laetrile was named by Dr. Ernest Krebs, Jr. It is crushed apricot pits. We praise the Lord that He gave us this knowledge and wisdom to correct my husband's body naturally. We will never say that the cancer is cured—just under control. All tests now show that there are no more active cancer cells. I am completely convinced that a good diet can go along way in preventing cancer and many other diseases.

The question is always asked, "Can you see any improvement in your family since you took sugar and white flour out of your diet and began eating all fresh and raw foods?" Let me give you a few statistics and perhaps these will answer the question. Two years before we started on natural foods, our young girls visited their pediatrician nine times. The next year, we were at the doctor ten times. The next year the score was only three times and this past year only *one* child went to the doctor *one* time. We have tried to build up our own natural immunities against disease by diet and vitamins. It has been at least a year and a half since either girl has had any antibiotics. If the girls ever need antibiotics, then they shall have it; but the body should be able to fight disease without it. The children get the flu once in awhile, but their bodies seem to snap back faster than other children. Colds are almost a rarity. We used to be an average family catching our share of everything. There has definitely been an improvement.

Some people think that because children get older, they are less susceptible to germs. I don't find this to be the truth.

Another benefit of a more natural diet is with hyperactive children. The diet in this book will help any child who has hyperactivity. Using honey has been known to help allergy—prone people.

Low blood sugar is not a problem to me any more. My list of jobs goes on and on and I am so grateful that I can see so much accomplished and not be tired.

CANCER PREVENTION AND CONTROL

The recipes given may be used as part of a wholistic Cancer Prevention Diet. For those people on a "Cancer Control" diet, caution is given for certain recipes. Some of the recipes will give an alternate ingredient, making it safer for a person who wants to keep his cancer under control.

BASIC INGREDIENTS USED IN RECIPES

ARROWROOT FLOUR—used to thicken liquids

BAKING POWDER—Rumford

BAKING SODA—Arm & Hammer or Cellu (from Natural Food Store)

BUTTER—real, unsalted or lightly salted with no preservatives or coloring. Used for greasing baking dishes, although Lecithin can be used. Butter should be kept to a minimum.

CHEESE—goat cheese or hard cheeses with no preservatives or coloring added. No processed or cheese spreads to be used.

DRIED FRUITS—unsulphured, sun dried and raw.

EGGS—fresh as possible. Try to buy from a farmer and find out what he feeds his chickens. Buy fertile eggs, if possible.

HONEY—raw, unpasteurized honey. Varieties depend upon locality. Orange blossom, clover and wildflower are good for baking. Tupelo should be used by Cancer Control patients. Try to buy directly from beekeeper.

MAYONNAISE—homemade or purchased. (Hain is good.)

MILK—goat's milk or non-instant, low fat powdered milk from a Health Food store.

MOLASSES—unsulphured, blackstrap.

NUTRITIONAL YEAST—primary yeast, also called brewer's yeast. It is a non-leavening yeast used to add Vitamin B to food.

NUTS—fresh, without preservatives, salt or oil added.

OATS—rolled oats.

OIL—safflower oil that is used in baking should be cold pressed, either Hain or Arrowhead Mills, not the kind from the grocery store. Other oils are olive, sunflower, sesame, and corn.

PEANUT BUTTER—Use only fresh ground peanut butter from the health food store, or a brand that contains just peanuts, no preservatives, or oils and is not hydrogenated. "Cancer Control" people should not use a lot of peanut butter.

SALT—use only sea salt or kelp.

VANILLA—pure vanilla extract.

VINEGAR—apple cider vinegar.

UNBLEACHED FLOUR—organic flour with the wheat germ still in it. Only to be used on special occasions. Arrowhead Mills makes a good unbleached flour.

WHOLE WHEAT FLOUR—stone ground fresh whole wheat flour. It is best to grind your own or buy from a reliable company. Sifting is optional.

WHOLE WHEAT PASTRY FLOUR—finer than whole wheat from soft winter wheat, good for pastries and cakes.

YEAST—baking yeast which is packaged, in cakes or in bulk.

YOGURT—unflavored, unsweetened, preferably home-made.

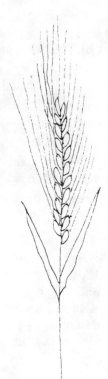

GENERAL SHOPPING LIST AND BEGINNING AMOUNTS

BEVERAGES:

Fruit juices—unsweetened, no added vitamins, several bottles
Red Zinger Tea—1 box

GRAINS:

Bran—1 pound
Whole Wheat Flour—5 pounds
Millet—1 pound
Rolled Oats—3 pounds
Brown Rice—1 pound
Bulgar—1 pound

VEGETABLES:

Dried Beans such as garbanzo, kidney, black beans, or navy beans—3 packages
Alfalfa seeds or mung beans for spouting—¼ pound
Fresh vegetables for recipes desired

CHEESE AND MEAT SUBSTITUTES:

Cheddar cheese and other unprocessed hard cheeses—3 pounds
Nuts—almonds, walnuts and cashews, all raw and unsalted—½ pound each
Peanut Butter—fresh ground, 1 pound
Seeds—sunflower and sesame, ½ pound each
Yogurt—either homemade or purchased unsweetened, 16 ounces

MISCELLANEOUS ITEMS:

Safflower Oil—1 quart
Carob Powder—1 pound
Raw Honey—½ gallon or 6 pounds
Tamari Sauce—1 bottle or 8 ounces
Unsweetened coconut—½ pound
Butter—1 pound
Sea Salt—1 pound
Non-instant, non fat dry powdered milk from the Natural Food Store—1 pound
Mayonnaise—either homemade or Hain, 1½ pints

If you don't want to purchase a general supply of ingredients, just buy whatever you need for each recipe.

LIQUID MEASURE CHART

Amounts	Equal
60 drops	1 teaspoon
1 teaspoon	⅓ tablespoon
1 tablespoon	3 teaspoons
2 tablespoons	1 fluid ounce
4 tablespoons	¼ cup or 2 ounces
5⅓ tablespoons	⅓ cup or 2⅔ ounces
8 tablespoons	½ cup or 4 ounces
16 tablespoons	1 cup or 8 ounces
3/8 cup	¼ cup plus 2 tablespoons
5/8 cup	½ cup plus 2 tablespoons
7/8 cup	¾ cup plus 2 tablespoons
1 cup	½ pint or 8 fluid ounces
2 cups	1 pint or 16 fluid ounces
1 pint	16 fluid ounces
1 quart	2 pints or 4 cups
1 gallon	4 quarts

CHAPTER 1

GRAINS AND CEREALS

GRAINS AND CEREALS

Most children start the day off with cereal. It probably is a very important part of their diet. Many children use cereal as a snack item. Consequently these children are eating a lot of cereal. Because of convenience, goofy cartoon characters or animals, and prizes, most of the cereal consumed by children is a dry boxed cereal rather than the cooked variety.

ARE YOU REALLY GETTING A
PRIZE IN YOUR CEREAL?

How many parents have taken their children to the grocery store and when they came to the cereal counter said, "All right, now I want you to pick out which cereal you want and then you are going to have to eat it this week. You decide which one." In fact, I am even guilty of this old trick to get the kids to pick what they like and then they will want to eat it. The choice is then made by which prize do they really want—will it be a magic trick? or a puzzle? or the miniature storybook? or the Star Wars characters? or the mystery prize? The choice is usually influenced by what television commercial the children have seen that week. Isn't it strange that we are a people so easily swayed by what someone says in a commercial.

When I started giving lectures, I had been inserting a little joke about cereal. I claimed that there was more nutrition in the box than in the cereal. After everyone gasped, I quickly commented that it was only my personal opinion. One day, someone came up to me and said, "You must have heard the nutritionist speak at our school." I had not heard the man speak, but was quite surprised to hear that scientists had just done a study and now have proven that there is more nutrition in the cardboard box than in the cereal. So, I guess the moral to this story is to eat the box and throw away the cereal.

SUGAR CONTENT IN CEREAL

Since we know that sugar is a "filler" and additive to almost everything, then it is no surprise that breakfast cereals are such a boost to the sugar industry. The average person has never bothered to figure out how much sugar is really in a box of cereal. They would be absolutely shocked to know that there is more sugar percentage wise in some cereals than there is in a chocolate candy bar. What exactly does this mean? Our children, or perhaps even you, would be getting less sugar if you ate a candy bar for breakfast rather than eating a bowl of cereal! That is truly shocking, especially when your mind has been trained to think that candy would be a terrible breakfast and cereal is so great. Bittersweet chocolate candy is about 47% sugar and plain milk chocolate candy is close to 57% sugar. Going down a list of cereals, I find that the sugar content goes as high as 56% in Sugar Smacks and Apple Jacks, with Froot Loops hitting 53% sugar. If that isn't bad enough, most people add more sugar when they start to eat the cereal.

LESS FIBER - MORE CANCER

Now that you have found out that packaged cereals are mostly sugar, did you ever wonder how much fiber is in them? After all, cereals and grains are eaten for their fiber content and nutrition. Fiber is roughage. It can pass through the intestine without being broken down by the body chemicals and enzymes. Fiber is what is left after the body gets through working the food over.

Our body needs twenty-four to twenty-five grams of fiber a day. The typical American eats about six to eight grams of fiber a day. Now we can understand why our bodies are plagued with disease. Fiber prevents bowel cancer, appendicitis, diverticular disease, constipation, hemorrhoids and cuts down on heart disease. It also prevents hiatal hernia. The reason that fiber can help in these diseases is that it works in the digestive system and in the breaking down of food. One way fiber helps to prevent heart attacks is by increasing the excretion of fats and cholesterols from the body. Fiber greatly reduces the amount of cholesterol secreted by the liver. There are at least 100,000 cases of bowel cancer in the United States yearly and 50,000 of these are fatal. Fiber is very important in the light of all this.

Foods that are high in fiber are the grains, seeds, nuts and many of the vegetables and fruits. Mango, apples and strawberries are highest in fiber in that order. Even bananas have fiber. All the leafy green vegetables are high in fiber along with carrots, peas, string beans and cabbage. Meat does not contain any fiber at all. The best source of fiber is raw wheat bran, which can be purchased from your local health food store. About three tablespoons a day should help anyone. Start out with a lesser amount until your body gets used to the bran. You can sprinkle it on cereal, put it in a drink, or eat it with other foods.

To give you an idea of how little fiber is in our cereals of today, let's start with the amount of fiber in a one ounce serving of raw milled bran. It contains 3.0 to 3.6 grams. Now, look at highest rated cereal according to fiber content - Kellogg's All-Bran, Bran Buds, and Nabisco's 100% Bran all contain between 1.8 and 2.3 grams of fiber per one ounce of cereal. That is almost less than half of the raw milled bran. Down at the bottom of the list are Sugar Pops, Sugar Frosted Flakes, Corn Total, Trix, Post Toasties, Cocoa Puffs, Country Corn Flakes. All these have a low fiber content of 0.1 to 0.2 grams per one ounce serving. All the other cereals fall somewhere in between the 0.1 and 2.3 grams of fiber content. What does all this mean to the average cereal eater? YOU ARE NOT GETTING WHAT YOU THINK YOU ARE GETTING.

I know the next question, "But what about all the grains we are eating in the cereal? Aren't they good for us?" Yes, if you could be sure that the grains were prepared like they were supposed to be, then your cereal would have a little bit to offer the world. The wheat, barley, oats, rice, and corn are all processed. Then, they are refined, or stripped of their fiber content. They are smashed, rolled, flattened out and puffed up. It is little wonder that they are lacking in nutrition and overloaded with sugar. Actually, the only nice thing about a box of cereal is the prize.

NATURAL GRAINS

If Bread is considered the "Staff of Life," then certainly grains must be the "Foundation of Life." The rest of the world lives on grains, but Americans have closed their eyes to them. Grains should be a very important part of our diet. In countries where the disease rate is low and cancer is unheard of, grains are high on the list of foods eaten. Overweight is not a problem with a balanced vegetable/grain diet. Grains have been considered good breakfasts, but with a little imagination, one can use them for a creative dinner. They should be stored in tight containers in a cool place, refrigerated or frozen. One of the best ways to make sure you are getting freshly ground grains, is to buy a grinder and mill your own grains.

The standard way to cook grains is to bring the water to a boil, and then add the grain. Stir once and when the water has returned to a boil, turn down the heat to low, cover, and let it cook for desired length of time. An alternate method of cooking grains is called the "Thermos Method." After rinsing the grain, place one cup grain into a wide mouth quart thermos. Add boiling water, leaving at least one inch space at the top for expansion. Stir with the handle of a wooden spoon. Screw lid on thermos and leave overnight at least eight hours. Another method is to place grains and water in crockpot. Turn on low and awaken to breakfast. Some grains can be soaked in water, and then are ready to eat.

BARLEY

Barley is a grain that needs plenty of water to grow and it holds much of the water. It is a difficult crop to hull and is pearled or rubbed to a rounded shape, sometimes. It is high in protein and minerals. Barley was used in Bible times as a basis of measurement. It is mentioned thirty-two times in the Bible. Probably the most famous mention of barley is in John 6:9-11 where a young boy gives the Lord Jesus his five barley loaves and two small fish to feed five thousand. HOW TO USE BARLEY? Add barley to your soups, substitute ¼ cup barley in any hot cereal that cooks at least 30 minutes, make puddings, and add it to a casserole or eat it for breakfast. Remember barley will increase four times the original amount when cooked.

COOKED BARLEY

1 cup barley   4 cups water

Rinse barley. Bring water to a boil and add barley. When water has returned to a boil, turn down heat to low, cover and let cook for 40 to 60 minutes. It will yield 4 cups cooked barley.

BARLEY FRUIT PUDDING

2 cups cooked barley	¼ teaspoon nutmeg
⅓ cup honey	½ teaspoon cinnamon
⅓ cup unsweetened	1 teaspoon vanilla
apple juice	¼ cup raisins
1 cup diced apples	¼ cup walnuts, chopped

Mix together all of the above ingredients and then bake in a buttered casserole dish for 30 minutes at 350 degrees. Serve with goat's milk, if desired.

BRAN

Bran contains B vitamins and is a fiber food. It is the outer covering of wheat and protects the wheat kernel. Bran is what is left over after flour milling. It is the natural ingredient which keeps things moving through your body. Read *The Save Your Life Diet* by Dr. David Reuben. This is an excellent book about fiber.

HOW TO USE BRAN? You can put it in almost everything. Add it to granola, cookies, muffins, casseroles, and breads. For a specific recipe, try BRAN MUFFINS in the Bread Chapter.

BUCKWHEAT

Buckwheat is not really a grain or wheat. It is a high fiber food from Siberia and Manchuria. It contains protein, B Vitamins and Rutin. The raw buckwheat flour is light in color, when roasted, it is dark. Buckwheat groats are reddish in color. HOW TO USE BUCKWHEAT? You can use the flour in breadmaking and buckwheat pancakes. The groats can be made into a casserole, added to soups, and made into a dish by themselves.

BUCKWHEAT GROATS

1 cup buckwheat groats   4 ½ to 5 cups water

Rinse the groats. Bring the water to a boil, add groats. Then allow the water to return to a boil, reduce the heat to low, cover and cook for 20 minutes.

BULGAR

Bulgar or cracked wheat is a staple of Eastern countries. It has the same nutritive value as whole wheat and is rich in protein and minerals. It has been par boiled and cracked. It is also spelled bulghur, borghul, bulgor, boulgor, boulgur, boulghour, burgul, burghul and burghol.

HOW TO USE BULGAR? It can be added to cooked cereals, casseroles, soups and stew. It can be a breakfast or when it is soaked, it can be used as a basis for salads.

COOKED BULGAR WHEAT

1 cup bulgar cracked wheat   2 cups water

Rinse bulgar. Bring water to a boil, add bulgar. Then allow water to return to a boil, reduce heat to low, cover and cook for about 15 minutes until soft.

SOAKED BULGAR WHEAT

1 cup bulgar cracked wheat   3 cups water

Rinse bulgar and drop into bowl with 3 cups of water. Allow it to sit for 2 hours. It will yield 3 cups ready-to-use bulgar.

BULGAR SALAD

1 cup bulgar soaked in 4 cups water until soft approximately 2 hours.
Add chopped vegatables:

    2 stalks celery, chopped
    4 red radishes, sliced
    ¼ cup green bell pepper, chopped
    10 raw mushrooms, sliced
    ½ medium onion, chopped
    ¼ cup raw zucchini squash, chopped
    ½ cucumber, chopped
    fresh parsley
    1 whole tomato, chopped
    1 carrot, sliced

Sprinkle with dressing:

    ¼ cup safflower oil
    1 tablespoon vinegar
    ¼ teaspoon sea salt

Serve:

    On a lettuce leaf topped with olives

BULGAR SPREAD

2 cups cooked bulgar
Add chopped vegetables:

    2 stalks celery
    ½ medium onion
    ¼ cup green bell peppers
    fresh parsley
    mayonnaise to make it spreadable

Optional:

    3 boiled eggs chopped

BULGAR PANCAKES

2 eggs	1½ cups whole wheat flour
2 tablespoons honey	2 cups cooked or soaked bulgar
¾ cup yogurt	¼ cup raisins-optional
¼ cup water	¼ cup ground walnuts-opt.
1 teaspoon vanilla	¼ cup diced apples-optional

Beat eggs, honey, yogurt, water, and vanilla. Slowly add flour and
bulgar. Add optional ingredients, if desired. Fry pancakes in very small
amount of safflower oil. Use medium to higher heat and flip over when
bubbles start to form.

BULGAR LOAF

3 cups soaked or cooked
bulgar
1 egg
¼ cup yogurt
Fresh parsley
10 mushrooms
1 medium onion

1 teaspoon garlic or 1
whole clove
1 teaspoon oregano
½ teaspoon sea salt
2 tablespoons tamari
3 tablespoons w.w. flour
1½ cups grated cheese—
reserve ½ cup for top

Mix all ingredients together and form into loaf. Place into buttered glass baking dish. Sprinkle cheese on top and bake at 350 degrees for 30 minutes.

CORNMEAL

Cornmeal is high in phosphorus. It is used quite extensively in South America and Mexico. Corn, as we know it, was not known in Bible days. Translators used the word "corn" in place of "wheat" or "grain."

HOW TO USE CORNMEAL? Make CORNBREAD from the Bread Chapter. Use small amounts in breadmaking and pie shells. Mix into casseroles. Make tacos and tortillas.

CORNMEAL COOKED

1 cup cornmeal   4 cups water

Bring water to a boil, drop in cornmeal. Allow water to return to a boil, reduce heat to low, cover and cook for 40 minutes.

MILLET

Millet is a non-glutenous lightly flavored grain which is a nutritional substitute for rice. It has been used as feed for animals and especially in bird seed.

HOW TO USE MILLET? It can be used wherever rice is needed or in combination with rice. It is also used in soups, casseroles, and with chop suey.

MILLET

½ cup millet   2 cups water

Rinse millet. Bring water to a boil, add millet and ½ teaspoon of sea salt, if desired. Then allow water to return to a boil, reduce heat to low, cover and cook for about 30 to 40 minutes until soft. Makes about 2 cups cooked millet. Fruit can be added to it.

MILLET LOAF

4 cups cooked millet
1 egg
2 tablespoons parsley
½ teaspoon garlic powder
½ teaspoon onion powder
½ teaspoon sea salt
1 teaspoon vegetable
   seasoning

10 mushrooms, sliced
1 medium onion, chopped
½ cup spaghetti sauce
2 tablespoons tamari sauce
3 tablespoons w.w. flour
green peppers

Add to the millet all the ingredients, except the cheese and ¼ cup spaghetti sauce. Place half of the mixture into a buttered glass dish approximately 10"x6". Shape into a loaf. Layer with sliced cheese. Add remainder of loaf. Top with the ¼ cup spaghetti sauce which was reserved and sprinkle grated Romano cheese. Decorate with sliced olives. Bake at 350 degrees for 30 minutes.

OATS

Oats have B vitamins, protein, phosphorus and iron. They are easy to use in many meals. Steel cut oats have to be cooked longer than rolled oats. Scotch oats are similar to steel cut oats and are very good, too. HOW TO USE OATS? Use oats as a breakfast cereal, in granolas, cakes, breads, and cookies. It can be blended into a flour.

OATMEAL

1 cup rolled oats   2 cups water

Bring water to a boil, add oats and a dash of sea salt. Then allow water to return to a boil, reduce heat to low, cover and cook for about 10 to 12 minutes. This will yield about 4 cups cooked oatmeal. Fruit can be added. Increase the recipe as follows to feed 2 adults and 2 children.

1½ cup rolled oats   3 cups water

SCOTCH OATS

1 cup scotch oats   4 cups water

Bring water to a boil, add oats and dash of sea salt. Then allow water to return to a boil, reduce heat to low, cover and cook for about 20 minutes until soft. Remove from heat and allow to stand an additional 2 minutes.

STEEL CUT OATS

½ cup steel cut oats   2½ cups water

Bring water to a boil, add oats and about ¼ teaspoon sea salt. Then allow water to return to a boil, reduce heat to low, cover and cook for at least 30 minutes or until soft.

GRANOLA

5 cups rolled oats
¾ cup honey
½ cup safflower oil
¼ cup water
1 cup coconut
2 cups w.w. flour

1 cup sunflower seeds
½ cup sesame seeds
½ cup cashews
1 cup bran
1 cup raisins—add after baking

Heat 5 cups rolled oats in a glass baking dish (13"x9"x2") at 350 degrees for 10 minutes. While the oats are baking, prepare liquid ingredients. Mix together honey, oil and water. Either use a blender or shake in a glass jar. Remove oats from oven and add coconut, sunflower seeds, sesame seeds, cashews, bran, and w.w. flour. Mix well and then add liquid. Mix again. Return to oven for 20 minutes. Stir about 3 times during the 20 minutes. Do not overbake. Add raisins after baking.

MARY'S ALMOND GRANOLA

5 cups rolled oats
½ cup honey
¼ cup safflower oil
1 cup sliced almonds (raw)

½ cup water
1 teaspoon pure almond extract
1 cup unsweetened coconut

Heat 5 cups rolled oats in baking dish at 350 degrees for 10 minutes. While oats are baking, prepare liquid ingredients. Mix tgether honey, oil and water. Either use blender or shake in glass jar. Remove oats from oven and add coconut and almonds. Then add liquid and mix well. Return to oven for 20 minutes. Stir 3 times during the 20 minutes.

CROCKPOT OATMEAL VARIATIONS

APRICOT OATMEAL

2½ cups water
1 cup rolled oats
1 cup apple juice

¼ teaspoon sea salt
½ cup dried apricots—cut up
¼ cup millet

Place all ingredients in a crockpot and turn on low. Leave overnight or approximately 8 hours.

VARIATION

Use ½ cup cut up apples and add ¼ cup raisins.

CINNAMON OATMEAL

3½ cups water
1½ cups rolled oats

½ teaspoon sea salt
1½ teaspoons cinnamon
⅓ cup raisins

Place all ingredients in a crockpot and turn on low. Leave overnight or approximately 8 hours.

RICE

Brown rice has the bran still on it as compared to white rice which has the bran or outer covering removed. Bran is loaded with Vitamin B. There are several varieties of rice—short, medium and long grain. The short grain is more glutenous than the others. Medium grain is tender and less glutenous than short grain. Long grain is lighter and has the most protein. Rice feeds one third of the human race. Wild rice is a different species than cultivated rice. It grows in the marshlands and is an expensive delicacy.

HOW TO USE RICE? Rice can be used in almost any dish-casseroles, soups, "meatless" loaves, rice pudding, Chinese dishes, and especially with chicken.

BROWN RICE

1½ cups long grain brown rice   4 cups water

Rinse the rice. Bring water to a boil, add rice and ½ teaspoon sea salt. Then allow water to return to a boil, reduce heat to low, cover and cook for about 40 minutes. Do not stir. It will yield about 3¾ cups cooked rice.

CROCKPOT RICE PILAF

3 cups water	¼ teaspoon rosemary
1½ cups long grain brown rice	¼ teaspoon marjoram
1 teaspoon sea salt	¼ teaspoon thyme
¾ cup chopped onion	1 pound fresh mushrooms,
2 teaspoons vegetable	sliced
seasoning in	2 tablespoons parsley
1 cup water or 1 cup	1 garlic clove
chicken stock	1 teaspoon coriander

Place all ingredients in crockpot, turn to low setting for 6 hours, or make on top of the stove, cooking on low setting for about 40 minutes.

CROCKPOT SPANISH RICE

1½ cups long grain brown rice	¼ cup green bell pepper
¼ cup olive oil	2 tablespoons parsley
3 cups tomato juice	1½ teaspoons sea salt
1½ cups water	1 clove garlic, cut up
1 onion	1 medium tomato, cut up
	10 sliced mushrooms

Place all ingredients in crockpot, turn to low setting for 6 hours. Compliment with a bean dish.

RYE

Rye is a grain that is ground into flour for bread making. It contains less gluten than wheat, and so whole wheat flour should be used with the rye in baking breads. Different variations of the bread are Russian Rye, Pumpernickel, Jewish Rye, and Sourdough Rye.

HOW TO USE RYE? Eat rye for breakfast, or make into breads.

CREAM OF RYE

1 cup rye flakes   3 cups water

Bring water to a boil, add rye flakes and ½ teaspoon sea salt. Boil for 3 minutes stirring. Turn off heat, cover and let stand off heat for 3 minutes.

WHOLE RYE GRAINS

1 cup whole rye   3 cups water

Rinse rye. Bring water to a boil, add rye and ½ teaspoon sea salt. Allow water to return to a boil, then reduce heat to low, cover and cook for one hour.

TRITICALE

Triticale is a new grain produced from a cross between wheat and rye. Triticale has 16.4% digestible proteins. It is about twice as large as regular wheat.

HOW TO USE TRITICALE? Experiment by using it in breads as you would wheat or rye.

WHOLE WHEAT

Whole wheat is the chief cereal crop for human beings and animals the world over. There are hundreds of varieties, but are classified usually as fall or winter wheat and spring wheat. The winter wheat or hard wheat is high in gluten and has 13% protein, while the spring or soft wheat is lower in gluten and has 8 to 10% protein. The hard wheat is better in breads and the soft wheat or pastry flour can be used in baking cakes and pastries. Many companies still use large granite stones to grind their flours, labeling the flour as "Stone Ground Whole Wheat." Whole wheat contains the wheat germ and the bran or covering of the wheat, whereas white flour has these two ingredients removed. Unbleached organic wheat flour with the wheat germ is much better to use than bleached white flour from the grocery store. The organic wheat flour has less Vitamin B content as compared to whole wheat flour, because of having less bran. Whole wheat is high in fiber, protein and Vitamin B. Cracked wheat is Bulgar.

HOW TO USE WHOLE WHEAT? Whole wheat berries can be used eaten as a cereal or used in casseroles. The flour can be used in bread making, cakes, cookies, and everywhere else flour is used.

WHEAT BERRIES

1 cup wheat berries   3½ cups water

Rinse berries. Bring water to a boil, add wheat berries and a dash of sea salt. Then allow water to return to a boil, reduce heat to low, cover and cook for about one hour.

CREAM OF WHEAT

⅔ cup wheat mush or flakes   3½ cups water

Bring water to a boil, add mush and dash of salt. Then turn to low for 15 minutes. It can be served with fruit.

WHOLE WHEAT PANCAKES

2 eggs   ½ teaspoon sea salt
¼ cup honey   ¾ cup yogurt
1 teaspoon baking soda   2 cups whole wheat flour
2 tablespoons safflower oil   ¾ cup water
                 1 cup blueberries-optional

Beat eggs, honey, soda, and oil. Add salt and yogurt. Gradually add flour with water. If desired, add blueberries. Fry in small amount of safflower oil.

VARIATIONS: 1 cup chopped apples for the blueberries.

Because fried foods are not good for anyone, this recipe should only be made occasionally.

WHEAT GERM

Wheat germ is the heart of the Wheat kernel and is very high in protein, vitamins and iron. The oil in the wheat germ will go rancid very quickly. In fact, the method of removing the wheat germ is difficult and unless a person can buy the wheat germ within one week after it is removed from the wheat; it has already gone rancid. For this reason, I feel that wheat germ can perhaps do more harm than good.

STEP-BY-STEP CHECK LIST FOR GRAINS AND CEREALS

Yes

1. I have stopped buying boxed cereals.   ____

2. I made oatmeal for breakfast one morning.   ____

3. I made granola for breakfast.   ____

4. I tried bulgar   ____

5. I tried millet.   ____

6. I have switched to brown rice.   ____

7. I now use whole wheat all the time.   ____

8. I have tried using a grain for supper, instead of meat.   ____

CHAPTER 2

BREAD, The Staff of Life

BREAD, THE STAFF OF LIFE

The age old adage that "bread is the staff of life" is almost a mockery when it comes to the squeezy bread from the grocery store. How sad to think that we are raising a generation of peanut butter and jelly white bread addicts. Giving soft spongy white enriched bread to a child is almost like giving him a beautiful box of candy loaded with arsenic. The wrapper is gorgeous, but the inside is deadly!

One day I was asked by my child's teacher to be a lunch room monitor. I enjoyed the chance to observe what came out of those lunchboxes. Out of 20 students, only 5 were eating whole wheat bread—all the rest were eating squeezy bread. Mentally I gave each of the lunches a grade. They all flunked! Each child had at least one or two sugar-laden poisonous foods. Some children had absolutely nothing of nutritive value in their lunch. The fruit was the only redeeming food, and many of those went into the garbage. Then I realized how alone my child was in a "sugar addicted" classroom where so much of life revolves around junk food.

When a person thinks of what makes up white bread, they usually think of finely ground beautiful white flour sifting through their hands. It may be wonderful to feel, but refining has all but ruined it. Refining is removing the outer part of the grain. This hull is loaded with vitamins and essential in breaking down the inside of the wheat. When you eat whole wheat flour, you are getting a whole product, not just half of the wheat berry.

After removing the B vitamins in refining, the manufacturers then bleach the flour so that it will have uniformity in color. Bleaching is done through chemicals. More poison is added.

Next, preservatives are put into the flour so that the shelf life will be from "here to eternity." Of course, these preservatives are chemicals that are poisonous to our bodies.

According to the U.S.D.A. Handbook No. 8, a loaf of whole wheat bread is much better for you than white bread.

Whole Wheat Bread 1102 calories		Enriched White Bread 1220 calories	
47.6	grams of protein	39.5	grams of protein
216	grams of carbohydrates	228	grams of carbohydrates
13	milligrams of niacin	10	milligrams of niacin
449	milligrams of calcium	318	milligrams of calcium
1000	milligrams of phosphorus	395	milligrams of phosphorus

Whole wheat bread has 11 percent fewer calories than white bread. It has less carbohydrates, more protein, more niacin, more calcium, and more phosphorus. Doesn't it seem sensible to choose whole wheat bread?

Enriched bread is really a joke. Quite a few years ago, the *Powers to Be* discovered that "white bread" wasn't even bread at all—just chemicals. And so they felt that Americans should have a little more than chemicals to eat. This brought about the idea of pumping the dough with synthetic vitamins and now we have "enriched" bread. In fact, 22 nutrients have been almost completely removed from the flour, with only 4 added back to the white flour. However, the vitamins they add aren't a drop in the bucket compared to the damage the so called "bread" does to your body.

In case you haven't heard, here is a partial list of what goes into squeezy bread: Sodium propionate, succinnylated monoglycerides, diacetly tartaric acid, calcium carbonate, calcium sulfate, lactylic stearate, ethoxylated diglycerides, sodium stearyl fumarate, potassium iodate and to top it off diacetyl iodate!

BIBLE REFERENCES

One of the first times bread is mentioned in the Bible is found in Genesis 18:5 and 6. Abraham tells his wife, Sarah, to make some bread for their visitors. The first baker is mentioned in Genesis 40.16. He is the chief baker for Pharoah and is in prison with Joseph. Instructions for making a certain kind of bread are given in Ezekiel 4:19, "Take thou also unto thee wheat, and barley, and beans, and lentiles, and millet, and fitches (herbs), and put them in one vessel, and take thee bread thereof . . ." And so one can see that for thousands of years, bread has been the staff of life.

Unleavened bread mentioned in the Bible is bread baked from unfermented dough. Leaven is symbolic of evil and generally not used in offerings or sacrifices.

DESSERT BREADS OR EASY BREADS

Some people are just born bread bakers, and others of us are not. Breads that contain fruit seem to be easier to make than the usual standard raised loaves. However, you may be gifted and have no problems whatsoever in turning out beautifully shaped, dark brown, sweet smelling, melt-in-your-mouth, deliciously flavored, homemade bread. Now I am sure you will be ready to make the staff of life with that introduction. If you need more information on flour, check the chapter on GRAINS before you begin to bake.

Be sure to use glass baking dishes, Corning Ware, or Pyrex. It is best to bake with glass instead of aluminum because the aluminum molecules start to break down when heated. Studies have shown that food cooked or baked in aluminum will contain aluminum. Stainless steel can also be used for cooking or baking. Grease the pans with butter or lecithin and dust with whole wheat flour.

Here is an easy, never-fail Banana Bread.

BANANA BREAD (1 Loaf)

⅓ cup butter	1 teaspoon baking soda
½ cup honey	½ teaspoon sea salt
2 eggs	1¾ cup whole wheat flour
2 large bananas	½ cup walnuts

Cream butter, raw honey, and eggs. Beat in bananas. Add soda, salt, and flour gradually. Then add broken walnut pieces. Butter and flour 1 glass loaf pan. Bake at 350 degrees for 55 to 60 minutes. The top will be cracked.

Now if your family is larger or you have a big appetite, here is the recipe for 2 loaves. It is changed slightly.

BANANA BREAD (2 Loaves)

⅔ cup butter	2 teaspoons baking soda
¾ cup honey	1 teaspoon sea salt
4 eggs	3½ cups whole wheat flour
5 bananas	1½ cups walnuts

Cream butter, raw honey, and eggs. Beat in bananas. Add soda, salt, and flour gradually. Then add broken walnut pieces. Butter and flour 2 glass loaf pans. Bake at 350 degrees for 55 to 60 minutes. The top will be cracked.

BANANA BLUEBERRY BREAD (1 Loaf)

½ cup butter	1½ cups whole wheat flour
⅔ cup honey	¼ teaspoon sea salt
2 eggs	½ cup rolled oats
2 bananas	1 cup blueberries
1 teaspoon baking soda	¾ cup walnut pieces

Cream butter, honey, and eggs. Beat in bananas. Slowly add soda, salt, and flour. When mixed good, add rolled oats. Now, very carefully, stir in fresh or frozen blueberries and broken walnut pieces. Butter and flour one glass loaf pan. Bake at 350 degrees for 55 to 60 minutes.

Cornbread goes very good with some meals. This is a sweet cornbread. If you like it unsweetened, leave out the honey.

CORNBREAD

1 egg	¼ teaspoon sea salt
2 tablespoons safflower oil	¼ teaspoon baking soda
¼ cup honey	½ cup whole wheat flour
½ cup yogurt	1 cup cornmeal

Mix egg, oil, honey, and yogurt. Add salt and soda. Gradually stir in flour and cornmeal. Batter will be thick. Butter and flour an 8"x10" glass baking dish. Bake at 425 degrees for 25 minutes until golden brown. You can make these into muffins, if you like.

Here is a recipe that is absolutely delicious. It really could be a dessert instead of a bread. Don't be scared off by the unusual ingredient—you can't taste it when it is baked.

MARZANNA'S ZUCCHINI BREAD

2 eggs	½ teaspoon baking powder
¾ cup honey	¼ teaspoon ground ginger
½ cup safflower oil	1½ cups whole wheat flour
½ teaspoon sea salt	1 medium zucchini squash,
½ teaspoon baking soda	grated
	½ cup walnut pieces

Beat eggs, honey and oil together. Stir in salt, soda, powder, ginger, and grated zucchini. (The zucchini should be about 1½ cups, locsely packed.) Mix in flour and broken walnuts. Butter and flour a loaf pan. Bake for 1 hour at 350 degrees.

If you are looking for a very nutritional bread, which is easy, try this power-packed goody.

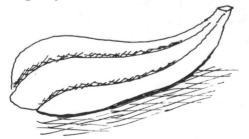

NUTRITIONAL BREAD

½ cup butter*
3 eggs
½ cup honey
½ cup molasses
½ cup orange juice*
1 cup grated carrots
½ teaspoon sea salt
2 teaspoons baking powder
¼ cup cashews, chopped

⅔ cup non-instant powdered milk
⅓ cup bran
¼ cup flax seed flour
2 cups whole wheat flour
¼ cup sunflower seeds, chopped
¼ cup walnuts, chopped
½ cup raisins

Mix butter, eggs, honey, unsulphured molasses, and juice. Add carrots, salt, and baking powder. Use ⅔ cup milk powder—do not make it liquid. Grind or blend the flax seeds to flour and add along with the bran. Slowly add the flour and remaining ingredients. Bake for one hour at 325 degrees in 2 buttered and floured glass bread pans or loaf pans.

*SUBSTITUTES

½ cup safflower oil for butter
½ cup apple juice for orange juice

MUFFINS

We place Bran Muffins at the top of the list. They are so good for us and yet easy to make.

BRAN MUFFINS

1 egg
2 tablespoons safflower oil
2 tablespoons honey
2 tablespoons molasses
¾ cup yogurt

1 teaspoon baking soda
¼ teaspoon sea salt
1 cup bran
¾ cup whole wheat flour
¼ cup water

Mix the first column of ingredients together. Add the second column. Butter and flour a muffin tin or use paper muffin holders. Bake for 30 mins. at 350 degrees. Cool before serving.

BRAN MUFFIN VARIATIONS

Add ½ cup raisins or sunflower seeds
Bake in 8x10 glass pan, cut into squares
Add 1 cup mashed ripe banana
Add 1 cup fresh or frozen blueberries
Add 1 cup finely chopped apples
Add ¼ teaspoon nutmeg, ½ teaspoon cinnamon and ½ cup chopped apples

BLUEBERRY MUFFINS

1 egg	¼ teaspoon sea salt
¾ cup yogurt	1 teaspoon baking soda
2 tablespoons safflower oil	1½ cups whole wheat flour
¼ cup honey	1 cup fresh or frozen blueberries

Mix the first column of ingredients. Add salt, soda, and flour. Gently fold in blueberries. There is one company which packages frozen fruits without sugar or preservatives. The name of the brand is "Big Valley." Bake the muffins for 30 mins. at 350 degrees. Be sure to butter and flour the pan well or use paper.

JELLY MUFFINS

2 eggs	½ teaspoon sea salt
½ cup honey	2 teaspoons baking powder
¾ cup crunchy peanut butter	2 cups whole wheat flour
¾ cup goat's milk*	¼ cup honey sweetened jelly

Mix the first four ingredients. *If you don't have goat's milk use ¾ cup liquid non-instant powdered milk. Add the dry ingredients. Butter and flour muffin tins. Place 2 tablespoons batter and 1 teaspoon jelly and then 2 more tablespoons batter. Bake at 400 degrees for 15 to 20 minutes.

RYE CARAWAY MUFFINS

1 tablespoon caraway seeds	½ teaspoon sea salt
2 tablespoons boiling water	2 teaspoons baking powder
1 egg	½ cup yogurt
3 tablespoons honey	¼ cup water
1 tablespoon molasses	¾ cup rye flour
¼ cup safflower oil	1 cup whole wheat flour

Soak the caraway seeds in boiling water for 5 minutes. Mix the egg, honey, molasses and oil together. Add the rest of the ingredients, mixing well after the flours. Pour seeds and water into the mixture. Butter and flour muffin tins and bake at 425 degrees for 20 minutes.

RAISED BREADS

Now that you have experimented with the easier breads, how about making a raised bread? The following is a basic recipe for whole wheat bread. When you start working with whole wheat flour, you'll see how much heavier it is than bleached white flour. If you prefer your bread to be a little lighter, you may use one half whole wheat flour and one half pastry flour or organic unbleached flour from the health food store. Flour is discussed in the chapter entitled, GRAINS AND CEREALS. Once you have tasted the hearty flavor of homemade whole wheat bread, you'll probably never go back to baking white bread again.

BARBARA'S NO-KNEAD WHEAT BREAD

Heat:
1 cup goat's milk
Add:
¾ cup safflower oil
½ cup honey, or ¼ cup depending upon sweetness desired
2 teaspoons sea salt
Dissolve:
2 tablespoons yeast
¾ cup warm water
Stir in:
3 eggs, slightly beaten
6 cups whole wheat flour

Heat the milk until bubbles form and remove from heat. Add the honey, oil and salt. Stir and allow to cool. Dissolve the yeast in the warm water in a large mixing bowl. Stir in the milk with the honey, oil, and salt along with the 3 eggs. You can mix this by hand or with an electric mixer. Add 4 cups of flour and beat at low speed until blended. Then beat at medium speed until mixture looks smooth, just about 2 minutes. Now add the additional 2 cups of flour with a wooden spoon. Then "squeeze" the dough by hand. This is done by placing your open hand into the dough and pulling your thumb and fingers together, allowing the dough to squeeze through your fingers. This helps break down the gluten in the wheat. Do this about 30 times. Cover the bowl and let it rise in a warm place for one hour. Then punch down the dough by hand and beat with a wooden spoon until the dough looks smooth or about 30 seconds. Lightly butter a 3 quart casserole bowl and place dough in bowl. Cover and let it rise again about 50 minutes to 1 hour. Before baking, cut a "+" in top of bread with a sharp knife. Bake at 350 degrees 45 to 50 minutes. Rub butter over top after baking, if desired. This makes 1 round loaf.

WHOLE WHEAT ROLLS

Dissolve:
2 tablespoons yeast or 2 packages
2 cups warm water
Add:
¼ cup melted butter
2 beaten eggs
⅓ cup honey
Blend:
2 teaspoons sea salt
6 cups whole wheat flour

Dissolve yeast in warm water. Then add butter to yeast. When melted, add eggs and honey. Mix well. Blend in the salt and flour. Knead dough on floured surface about 5 minutes. Place dough in a buttered bowl, cover and let rise in a warm place until doubled or about 45-60 minutes. Punch down the dough and form small balls. Place the balls on a buttered baking sheet about 3 inches apart. Cover and let rise again 30 to 45 minutes until light and doubled. Bake at 400 degrees for about 12 to 15 minutes.

RYE ROLLS

Dissolve:
2 tablespoons yeast or 2 packages
2 cups warm water

Add:
¼ cup melted butter
2 beaten eggs
⅓ cup honey

Blend:
1 tablespoon sea salt
4 cups rye flour
2 cups whole wheat flour

Soak:
¼ cup caraway seeds in
¼ cup boiling water and pour off water when adding seeds

Dissolve yeast in warm water. Then add butter to yeast. When melted, add eggs and honey. Mix well. Blend in salt and flour. Pour water off caraway seeds and add seeds to dough. Then knead dough on a floured surface about 5 minutes or until smooth. Form 2 inch balls and place about 3 inches apart on a buttered baking sheet. Place in warm spot, covered until dough doubles in size or about 1 hour. Bake at 400 degrees for 10 to 12 minutes.

When baking with rye or oat flour, it is necessary to use some gluten flour or whole wheat flour. Rye and oat flour do not contain very much gluten and these breads turn out quite heavy, if used alone.

RYE BREAD

Dissolve:
3 tablespoons yeast or 3 packages
2 cups goat's milk or non-instant, non fat dry milk, scalded, then cooled
   to lukewarm

Add:
2 tablespoons molasses
1 egg

Mix:
1 tablespoon sea salt
½ cup nutritional yeast
5½ cups rye flour
½ cup whole wheat flour
2 tablespoons caraway seeds

Heat the milk until hot, then cool. When lukewarm, dissolve the yeast in it. Add the molasses and egg. Gradually add the nutritional yeast, sea salt and flours. Mix well. Then knead on a floured surface about 5 minutes or until smooth. Place in a buttered bowl, cover and let rise in a warm place about 1 hour until doubled in size. Punch down and divide in half. Form 2 round loaves. Place on a buttered baking sheet, cover and return to warm place to rise until doubled in size or about 1 hour. Bake at 375 degrees for 40 minutes.

PITA POCKET BREAD

Dissolve:
    2 tablespoons yeast or 2 packages in
2½ cups warm water
Add:
    1 teaspoon honey
1½ teaspoons sea salt
    1 tablespoon safflower oil
    3 cups whole wheat flour added now; 3 cups added later

After all ingredients are mixed well, work in the additional 3 cups whole wheat flour. Knead for 5 or 10 minutes. Divide the dough into 20 pieces, rolling with rolling pin into 4" rounds, ¼" thick. Place on ungreased baking sheet, cover and let rise in warm place for about 2 hours. Start in bottom rack of oven for 5 minutes at 500 degrees. Then move bread to higher shelf and bake until puffed up about 3 to 5 minutes. When cooled, slice in half. Bread will have a pocket to put sandwich filling in. Check the chapter on SANDWICHES.

If you can't seem to make yeast breads, then try the following recipe. It really does work and it is so easy.

OATMEAL BREAD

1½	cups boiling water	1½	tablespoons safflower oil
1	cup rolled oats	1	tablespoon yeast
1	teaspoon sea salt	¼	cup water
⅓	cup honey	3½	cups whole wheat flour

Pour boiling water over the oats. Add the salt, stir and cool. Dissolve the yeast in warm water. Then to the oats, add honey, oil, and yeast. Gradually stir in flour. Knead for 5 minutes on floured surface. Butter a large bowl and place dough in bowl. Allow the dough to rise in a warm place until doubled in size, about 1 hour. Then punch down and put into a buttered glass loaf pan. Let it rise again for one hour. Bake at 375 degrees for 50 minutes.

The next recipe is only for festive occasions and contains organic unbleached flour. You will find out more about flours in the chapter, GRAINS AND CEREALS. Since these Cinnamon Rolls really taste like the "sugary ones," it is best to make them just once in awhile. They are not only time consuming to make, but very rich. You had better stay away from these goodies if you are on a cancer control diet.

CINNAMON ROLLS

Dissolve:
  2 tablespoons yeast or 2 packages
  ¼ cup lukewarm water

Add together in separate bowl:
  1 cup scalded goat's milk or non-instant milk
  ½ cup butter
  ¼ cup honey
  2 teaspoons sea salt
     Cool

Mix with above ingredients:
2 eggs
  yeast and water

Add gradually:
  2 cups whole wheat flour
2½ cups organic unbleached white flour

Turn dough onto floured surface and knead until smooth. Place dough in buttered bowl, cover, and let rise 45 to 60 minutes in a warm place until doubled. Punch dough down and let it rest for 10 minutes. Roll out one half of the dough into a rectangle. Spread with cinnamon honey filling and then roll like a jelly roll. Cut into 1 to 1½ inch slices place in buttered pan so they barely touch. Cover and let rise in warm place for about 30 minutes or until doubled. Prepare rest of dough. Bake at 350 degrees for about 50 to 60 minutes until rolls are browned. Pour glaze over top.

CINNAMON HONEY FILLING

1 cup honey	2 teaspoons cinnamon
1 tablespoon grated orange rind	⅔ cup raisins
	1 cup chopped pecans
2 tablespoons orange juice	2 tablespoons melted butter

Combine all of the above and spread over dough.

CINNAMON ROLL GLAZE

½ cup honey	1 tablespoon butter
1 tablespoon grated orange rind	

Simmer all of the above for about 5 minutes. Pour over cinnamon rolls. Sprinkle with chopped pecans, if desired.

CRACKERS

Crackers are easy and fun to make. Even the children can help. They are also fast. Here is a simple recipe for whole wheat crackers. With a little imagination, you can make all kinds of tasty crackers.

BILL'S WHOLE WHEAT CRACKERS

2 cups whole wheat flour
1 teaspoon sea salt
½ cup sesame seeds
¼ cup bran
¼ cup safflower oil
¾ cup cold water

Mix the dry ingredients together. Slowly add the oil and water and continue stirring. Place the dough on a piece of waxed paper. Place another piece of waxed paper over the top and roll the dough out very thin. Butter a cookie sheet. Pull off the top layer of waxed paper and flip the crackers over onto the baking sheet. Pull off the other piece of paper. Cut with a sharp knife before baking. Bake at 400 degrees for 15 minutes, but watch closely so they aren't overdone.

WHOLE WHEAT VARIATIONS

Eliminate the bran and add:

¼ cup dried onion flakes or
3 ounces cheddar cheese, grated

BREAD STICKS

8 slices of whole wheat bread
2 tablespoons butter
3 tablespoons honey
2 tablespoons sesame seeds

Melt butter and honey together. Brush on bread. Sprinkle with sesame seeds. Cut bread into 4 lengths or sticks and bake 8-10 minutes until crisp at 400 degrees.

VARIATIONS

Use peanut butter in place of butter
Sprinkle cinnamon on top of original recipe

STEP-BY-STEP CHECK LIST FOR BREADS

Yes

1. I have read the label of the bread I am now eating.   _____

2. I have stopped eating white squeezy bread and am
    now eating whole wheat bread.   _____

3. I have made sandwiches for the family out of whole
    wheat bread.   _____

4. I have tried making one of the dessert breads or easy
    breads.   _____

5. I have tried cornbread or muffins to be
    eaten with our meal.   _____

6. I have purchased whole wheat or grain bread from a
    health food store.   _____

7. I have found a whole wheat bread that contains no
    sugar, no preservatives, and no white flour.   _____

8. I have tried one of the raised breads.   _____

9. I have now turned down squeezy white bread when
    eating out.   _____

CHAPTER 3

FRUIT AND VEGETABLES

FRUIT

One of the best sources of natural sugar is fruit. Figs are mentioned throughout the Bible. Their first appearing was literally "on" Adam and Eve in the form of fig leaves. Later, figs are used as a peace offering and even in healing as recorded in II Kings 20:7. The fig tree was highly prized and it was a symbol of prosperity. The figs are dried for preservation and are a staple article of food in southern Europe.

Likewise, pomegranates are easily grown in the Palestine area and grow wild in northern Africa and western Asia. The English name means apple with many seeds. Pomegranates are mentioned several times in the Bible. In Exodus 28:34, they were used in the hem of the high priest's robe as decorations. Solomon's temple had a double row of one hundred pomegranates carved in it. In Deuteronomy, they are given in a list to describe the Promised Land, Canaan.

Apples aren't mentioned quite as frequently as the first two fruits listed. Solomon refers to them in Song of Solomon. The old saying that someone is the "apple of my eye" is found in Deuteronomy 32:10.

Grapes are referred to throughout the Bible as the "vine." Noah planted a vineyard recorded in Genesis 9:20. Grapes grow easily in southern Europe, western Asia, south of the Caspian Sea, and throughout Egypt. There are several varieties of grapes and they can be eaten fresh or dried as raisins. The Promised Land had such large clusters of grapes that it took two men to carry them on a pole.

Muskmelons and watermelons are grown in immense quantities in Egypt. The Children of Israel remembered eating them as recorded in Numbers 11:5.

Olives grow on trees throughout southern Europe. The oil made from pressed olives has many uses. The olive tree, olive and oil are mentioned quite frequently in the Bible. The first appearing is in Genesis 8:11 where a dove returns to Noah with an olive branch. Now it is symbolic of peace. The olive was also a symbol of prosperity, divine blessing, beauty and strength. At the Olympic games in Greece, the victor's crown was composed of olive leaves.

Fruits should be eaten fresh and raw. They lose some of their vitamin content when cooked or baked. Put a large fruit bowl in plain sight for all to help themselves. Children should be encouraged to choose fruit rather than cookies or other snacks.

If dried fruits are purchased, get the unsulphured. Sulphur is an additive to preserve color. Children love to snack on dried fruits and they keep a long time in the refrigerator. Here is a suggested list of some dried fruits you could buy:

DRIED FRUITS
Apple
Appricot
Coconut
Dates
Figs
Pears
Pineapple
Prunes
Raisins

A person can eat too much fruit and raise his blood sugar level. Persons with hypoglycemia have to be cautious of some fruit because there is too much natural sugar content in the fruit. This causes the pancreas to react and sends extra insulin into the blood stream. The insulin takes all the natural sugar out of the blood stream and what's left is a very tired person. Moderation is the key to eating fruit. Persons with low blood sugar should stay away from dates and grapes.

Fruit should be eaten between meals and can be used as dessert. My family will go for weeks without any baked dessert, just enjoying whatever fruit is in season.

BERRIES

Blackberries
Blueberries
Boysenberries

Cranberries
Raspberries
Strawberries

MELONS

Cantaloupe
Casaba

Honey Dew
Muskmelon
Watermelon

SWEET FRUITS

Bananas
Cherries (sweet)
Figs

Grapes (sweet)
Mangos
Papayas
Persimmons

SLIGHTLY SWEET FRUITS

Apricots
Cherries (tart)
Grapes (tart)

Nectarines
Peaches
Plums

ACID FRUITS

Apple (sour)
Grape (sour)
Grapefruit
Lemon
Lime
Orange

Peach (sour)
Pineapple
Plum (sour)
Pomegranate
Tangelo
Tangerine

SLIGHTLY ACID FRUITS

Apple (sweet)
Apricot
Cherry (sweet)
Fig (fresh)
Huckleberry

Mango
Papaya
Peach (sweet)
Pear
Plum

WATERMELON SALAD

½ watermelon   ½ cantaloupe or
½ honey dew   muskmelon

Dig out all the watermelon and scallop the edges all the way around the watermelon. Make watermelon balls, honey dew and cantaloupe balls and put them all back into the watermelon basket. It's a wonderful way to serve fruit for guests in the summertime.

FRUIT SALAD

2 bananas   yogurt
2 stalks celery, chopped   honey to taste
   bunch of grapes   ½ cup walnuts

Mix the fruit (grapes cut in half), celery, and walnuts. Add enough yogurt to moisten the fruit and honey to taste.

AMBROSIA

3 oranges, peeled, cut into bitesize chunks
2 grapefruit, peeled, cut into bitesize chunks
1 tablespoon unsweetened coconut

WALDORF SALAD

2 cups diced unpeeled apples   ⅓ cup broken walnuts
½ cup diced celery   mayonnaise to moisten

Combine apples, celery and walnuts. Use enough mayonnaise to moisten or yogurt with honey to taste.

CRANBERRY RELISH

2 cups cranberries   1 whole apple
1 sweet orange   ¼ cup honey   ½ cup walnut pieces

Wash cranberries. In a blender place a small amount of cranberries, prepared orange and cored apple. Repeat process until cranberries, orange and apple are blended. Add honey and walnut pieces.

VEGETABLE MEASUREMENTS

ASPARAGUS—1 pound, 15-22 stalks.................2 cups cooked

BEANS:

    Dried Beans—1 pound.........................2½ cups dried or
                            5 to 7½ cups cooked
    Dried Limas—1 cup...........................2½ cups cooked
    Dried Red Beans—1 cup.......................2½ cups cooked
    Dried Red Beans—12 ounces ....2 cups cooked
    Dried White Beans—1 cup.......................3 cups cooked
    Dried Black Beans—12 ounces....................2 cups dried,
    Dried Garbanzo Beans—12 ounces.................2 cups dried
    Dried Lentils—12 ounces ....2 cups dried
    Green or Waxed Beans—1 pound in pod............3 cups cooked
    Lima Beans—1 pound in pod............⅔ cups shelled, uncooked

BEETS—1 pound, 4 medium ....2 cups cooked, diced

BROCCOLI—1 bunch............................1½ to 2½ pounds

BRUSSELS SPROUTS—1 pound ....3 cups cooked

CABBAGE—1 pound...................3½ to 4 cups shredded raw,
                                    2½ cups cooked

CARROTS—1 pound, 7 or 8................2¼ cups diced uncooked,
                                     2 cups cooked

CAULIFLOWER—2 pound head.....................3 cups cooked

CELERY—1 pound ....3 cups diced raw,
                                    2 cups cooked

CORN—4 medium ears...................................1 cup cut

EGGPLANT—1 pound ....11 slices of ½ inch
                         4½ cups, diced or uncooked
                         1¾ cups, diced, cooked

MUSHROOMS— 1 pound.............35 to 45 medium mushrooms
    10 medium ....1 cup, sliced

ONIONS—1 pound dry ....3 large onions
    1 medium.......................................½ cup chopped

PARSNIPS—1 pound.................................4 medium
                              2½ cups cooked, diced

PEAS:

    Green Peas—1 pound ....1 cup cooked
    Split Peas—1 pound ....2 cups uncooked
                                    4 cups cooked

POTATOES:
    White Potatoes—1 pound..................... 3 medium potatoes
                                              2½ cups diced, cooked
    Sweet Potatoes—1¼ pounds............ 2¾ cups cooked, mashed

RUTABAGAS—1 pound .... 2 ⅔ cups cooked, diced
                                              2 cups mashed

SPINACH (or other greens)—1 pound .... 1½ to 2 cups cooked

SQUASH:
    Summer Squash—2 pounds .... 2 cups cooked, mashed
    Hubbard Squash—5 pounds.............. 5 cups cooked, mashed

TOMATOES—1 pound........................ 4 small to medium
                                              4 slices to each tomato

TURNIPS—1 pound .... 3 or 4 cups

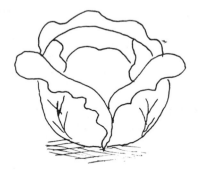

BIBLE REFERENCES TO VEGETABLES

Different vegetables are mentioned throughout the Bible and especially in connection with the Children of Israel remembering what was eaten in Egypt. In Numbers ll:5, they recalled, "We remember the fish, which we did eat in Egypt freely; the cucumbers, and the melons, and the leeks, and the onions, and the garlick:" The "bitter herbs" referred to in Exodus 12:8 is commonly thought of as dandelion greens or endive. Incidentally, dandelion greens have 50% more vitamin A than any other fruit or vegetable. It also contains certain B vitamins, calcium and phosphorus. Lentils were quite popular in Genesis 25:34 when Jacob sold his pottage of lentils to Esau for his birthright. Lentils have a food value as compared to sirloin steak. They have more protein, less fat, more calcium, phosphorus, iron, thiamine, riboflavin, vitamins A and C, than steak. Beans are mentioned in II Samuel 17:27-28 and Ezekiel 4.9.

In the Old Testament, Daniel places vegetables in high regard. Because the King's meat had been dedicated to idols, making it defiled, Daniel chose to eat "pulse" or vegetables alone. The vegetable food proved to be more than adequate for Daniel and his friends—"their countenances appeared fairer and fatter in flesh than all the children which did eat the portion of the king's meat." (Daniel 1:15) Now that word "fatter" means that their flesh was better looking than the others who ate the king's meat.

OUR WONDERFUL PLANT WORLD

Since the plant world was designed to sustain man, it seems only natural that we delve into vegetables full force. Vegetables contain vitamins, minerals and proteins which we need to live. I would advocate eating as many raw vegetables as possible. In her book, HOW I CONQUERED CANCER NATURALLY, Eydie Mae Hunsberger explains that her entire diet is raw food. I am thoroughly convinced that anyone with any disease at all would be well, if they would only follow Eydie Mae's diet. It's fantastic. Unfortunately, most people are too stubborn to give up their "favorites" for a healthy body. So many good enzymes in vegetables are lost whenever they are cooked. Eating food raw works the saliva glands, the gums, and helps place valuable enzymes into the digestive system. Vegetables add fiber to the diet.

Most people eat less than one dozen different vegetables. Some people may venture as far as eating two dozen vegetables. Would you believe that there are over two hundred types of vegetables grown commercially in America? Why are we so stuck in our eating habits? Just because Mother cooked this way doesn't mean that we have to carry on the tradition. Be bold—be inventive! Branch out into a new field. Take the best of Mother's cooking and then find out how your grandmother cooked. Then ask your neighbor what vegetables her family eats and how she fixes them. Now you have the better of two worlds. Just keep adding to that vegetable list. Don't be afraid to try a new vegetable.

It is best to eat vegetables RAW instead of cooked because of the loss of enzymes. When enzymes are heated above 122 degrees Fahrenheit, they are destroyed. Twenty to forty-five percent of the vitamins are lost within the first four minutes of cooking.

If you don't want to eat the vegetables raw, then steam them. They should be crisp. You can buy a little stainless steel steaming basket that will fit in any size pan. Just place water in the bottom, keeping the level one fourth inch below the bottom of the steamer. Drop in the basket with the vegetables, cover and heat water to boiling. Within ten minutes or less, most vegetables are ready to eat.

If you get tired of this method, try baking the vegetables at 350 degrees or lower with a small amount of water. You are in a sense steaming them in the oven. Some vegetables can be "quick fried" the greaseless way. Instead of frying in butter or oil, try using 2 tablespoons water. Skillet dishes don't need grease, actually many different liquids would work. How about saving the water from your steamed vegetables and use as a basis for Chop Suey? You would have more vitamin content if you would drink it after the vegetables have been steamed, but you could save it for soup stock. Also you can blend raw vegetables, add water and heat quickly for a fast soup.

Try to eat the whole vegetable—peeling and all. If you see wax on the outside, then peel it. If you think the vegetables were sprayed, then peel it. Try to wash all vegetables very thoroughly.

Buy your vegetables from a private farmer if possible. Try to find an organic farmer, one who doesn't use poisonous sprays and deadly chemicals. If you know where your food comes from, you'll feel better about eating it. I am so thankful my parents have a garden and share their vegetables with my family. I can be assured of no poison on their vegetables.

Another good source of fresh vegetables and all other supplies is a co-op. These unique stores are scattered around the country and can be found in almost every large city. In a co-operative store, you become a member and have the advantage of better prices than in a regular natural food store by ordering in bulk. If there isn't one in your area, why not start one? There are several good books published explaining all about co-ops that would be very helpful.

Of course, the best way to know your vegetables is to GROW THEM YOURSELF. How wonderful to walk outside and pick what you want for supper. There are several good books and magazines explaining organic farming. The use of worms to aerate the soil and replace minerals has come into prominence. Also beneficial insects such as lady bugs are being used to get rid of harmful insects. If you don't have the room for a garden, or you have a "brown thumb," then try buying your vegetables from the best source.

When you harvest your garden and can't eat it all, then you can freeze or can the leftovers. Of course, fresh vegetables are the best, but your own vegetables frozen or canned are second best. At least you know what you have done to them.

I am sure that you won't be able to buy all your vegetables fresh. There are always a few that are hard to find. Then buy the dried ones. Or if you absolutely need that vegetable, buy it frozen. In my area, it's hard to find fresh peas at a reasonable cost, so I must resort to frozen peas. However, they are eaten infrequently, so the loss is not too great. It is hard to know the processing in frozen vegetables and of course, vitamin content is lost through freezing.

"Tin Canned" vegetables are definitely out. If you could follow those vegetables through the canning factory, you would never open another can in your life. Besides having too much salt and sugar in them, the vegetables are so overcooked there can't be any vitamin content left. Studies have shown that the can itself somehow seeps into the vegetables. Just imagine tiny particles of "tin" accumulating in the body. Our can opener is stored away. It is only used on special occasions to open a can of black olives. If I could find the olives in bottles, I would give away my can opener.

The following list contains 97 Vegetables and how to use them. All of them can be eaten raw, but some taste a little better when steamed. Our preference is to steam a vegetable rather than cook it.

HOW TO USE 97 VEGETABLES

ARTICHOKES, GLOBE—These have compact leaves or scales.
Better Eaten—Cooked or Steamed

> Prepare—Remove any brown leaves and cut one inch off the top. Cut off each point with a scissors. Rinse the artichoke and if you do not want the scales to spread out, tie a string around it.
>
> Cook—Use a large pot and heat enough water to cover artichokes. Allow one per person. Add to the water 1 teaspoon sea salt, 1 garlic clove, 1 tablespoon Safflower Oil, and 1½ teaspoons lemon juice for each artichoke. After water boils, add the artichokes and reduce the heat to low. Cook uncovered for about 30 to 40 minutes. When leaves pull out easily, then the artichokes are finished. Carefully remove them and turn over to drain. To eat, remove each leaf and dip into melted butter, or a sauce, and draw between the teeth. The fiber leaf will be left. Remove the fuzzy part over the heart and eat the inside or "heart" of the artichoke.

Steam—18 to 20 minutes.
Ways to use—Serve as you would any vegetable.

ARTICHOKES, JERUSALEM—An underground tuber of the sunflower. It is not related to the globe artichoke. It contains no true starch, is low in calories, rich in phosphorus, iron and Vitamin A.

Better eaten—Raw or steamed, but there are more vitamins and minerals when eaten raw.
> Prepare—Scrub and scrape the skin with a brush. Wash thoroughly.
> Cook—Cook in boiling water for about 10 minutes.
> Steam—6 to 8 minutes.
Ways to Use—Slice and use raw in salads. Slice and use like water chestnuts in Chop Suey. Use instead of potatoes.

STEAMED JERUSALEM ARTICHOKES

1 pound of Jerusalem Artichokes—wash, scrape or peel and slice. Steam in a basket steamer for 8 minutes. Serve with butter, sea salt, and parsley. It will serve 3 or 4 people.

AVOCADO—This is a fruit, not a vegetable and is high in protein and potassium. Use it raw in salads or add lemon juice.

ASPARAGUS—Smooth, round, tender green spears with closed tips. It has Vitamin A.

Better eaten—Raw or cooked. It has more vitamins and minerals when eaten raw.

Prepare—Wash thoroughly and break off the tough end.

Cook—Boil water, place asparagus standing up in pan, cook uncovered for 5 minutes. Then cover and cook 7 to 10 minutes until stalks are tender.

Steam—8 to 12 minutes.

Ways to use—Slice complete raw stalk for salads or just use tips in salad. Dip the raw tips in yogurt dip. Steam asparagus and place cheese on them to melt.

BAMBOO SHOOTS—These are not vegetables, but grasses. The young tender shoots are used in Chinese cooking.

BEANS, FRESH GREEN BEANS—This is probably the most popular of all beans. It contains Vitamin A and potassium.

Better eaten—Steamed or raw

Prepare—Wash thoroughly and remove one end. Leave beans whole, or snap in half or small pieces. They can be cut lengthwise for French style beans.

Cook—In about one inch or so of boiling water with sea salt until tender or 10 to 15 minutes. (1 pound)

Steam—7 to 10 minutes

Ways to use—Put sliced almonds in beans when serving them. Combine with other vegetables.

GREEN BEANS AND POTATOES

½ quart water

4 potatoes, scrubbed,
   quartered, with peelings on

1 tablespoon parsley

1 pound fresh green beans

1 teaspoon sea salt

1 medium onion, chopped

1 clove garlic, chopped

Boil the potatoes in water and salt. When half cooked, add rest of the ingredients. Cook until potatoes are finished and green beans are tender. Wax beans can be added to this recipe, if desired.

BEANS, WAX—These are yellow beans and can be fixed the same way green beans are cooked.

BEANS, LIMA—These can be purchased fresh in the pod, dried, or frozen. There are several varieties, Fordhook, baby limas, and butter beans are some of them. They are high in potassium and are a good source of nitrilosides.

Better eaten—Young tender beans can be eaten raw. Others can be steamed.

Prepare—Shell fresh limas, or wash dried limas.

Cook—For fresh limas, cook until tender in small amount of water, approximately 25 to 30 minutes.

For 1 pound dried limas, bring 1 quart of water to a rolling boil. Drop in limas, 2 bay leaves, and turn off heat. Replace lid and allow beans to sit for one hour. Then turn on medium heat and cook for one more hour or until tender.

Steam—10 minutes for fresh or frozen limas.

Ways to use—Use with other vegetables such as green beans, carrots, or mushrooms. Make succotash with corn. Serve creamed with a little butter and goat's milk.

BEANS, DRIED—These have the highest protein content, 20% to 24%, of all food crops. Beans help keep much of the world alive. There are 24 varieties. They have B vitamins, calcium, magnesium, iron and phosphorus.

Better eaten—Cooked

Prepare—Rinse thoroughly and pick out any dirt or rocks.

Cook—Boil one quart of water for 1 pound of beans. After water comes to a rolling boil, drop in rinsed beans with 2 bay leaves. Turn off heat and cover. Resume cooking on medium heat after one hour. Cook until tender, approximately one to two hours, depending upon the beans.

Ways to use—Use in soups, or casseroles. Use with rice or over rice. Use cold in salads. Mash for spreads or dips by adding mayonnaise.

Aduzki—Small red bean, good for sprouting.

Black—Sometimes called Spanish beans, used in turtle soup.

Black Eyed
Peas—Sometimes called Cow Peas and have a small black eye. Called black eye beans after drying.

Garbanzo Sometimes called Chick Peas. Used in Spanish cooking. It is a round bean larger than a pea. It can be soaked and eaten cold.

Kidney—Dark red kidney-shaped bean used a lot in Spanish cooking and chili. There is also a light red kidney bean used the same way.

Lima—White lima

Mung—Used for sprouting

Navy—Small white bean used in baked beans and bean soup.

Northern—A little larger bean than a Navy bean used in baked beans and soup. Sometimes called Great Northern.

Pea—Smallest of white beans used in soups.

Pinto—A small speckled bean with the highest protein content of any other bean.

Pink—Used in Spanish cooking.

Soy—Used in many dishes to replace meat. Good for sprouting. Soybeans have purposely been avoided in this book. People on a cancer control diet should not eat soy products because it has an enzyme inhibitor. Tamari Sauce, however is made so that it does not slow down the enzyme processes. "Tofu" is a custard-type food from soymilk.

BEAN SOUP

10 cups water
½ cup lima beans
½ cup lentils
½ cup navy beans
½ cup garbanzo beans
3 bay leaves
¼ cup bulgar

1 teaspoon garlic or clove
1 teaspoon sweet basil
2 teaspoons sea salt
2 medium onions, chopped
2 medium carrots, sliced
2 celery stalks, chopped
1 tablespoon parsley

Bring the water to a boil, drop in the beans and bay leaves, then shut off the heat. Allow beans to sit for one hour, covered. Turn heat on and add all other ingredients. Cook for approximately two hours until beans are tender. You may cook in a crock pot on low for 6 hours.

BLACK BEAN/RICE SOUP

2 cups black beans or
   12 ounces
3 cups water for beans
½ cup lentils
2 bay leaves
½ cup brown rice

1 teaspoon sea salt
1 medium onion, chopped
1 garlic, minced
1 celery stalk, chopped
7½ cups liquid (water, bean
   juice, chicken stock, etc.)

Heat 3 cups of water for the black beans. When water boils, drop in black beans and bay leaves. Turn off heat, cover and allow beans to sit for 1 hour. Resume cooking on medium heat. Add rest of the ingredients. Cook approximately 2 hours. If water is used for the 7½ cups liquid, add vegetable seasoning. If you use a crockpot, cook on high for 4 hours, or low for 6 hours. You may adjust liquid in soup to serve your family.

GARBANZO BEANS AND RICE

3 cups water
1½ cups brown rice
1 cup water with 2 tsps.
   vegetable seasoning or
1 cup chicken stock
1 teaspoon sea salt
2 cups garbanzo beans

¾ cup chopped onion
10-12 musrooms, sliced
2 tablespoons parsley
1 teaspoon garlic or clove
1 teaspoon coriander
¼ teaspoon of rosemary,
   majoram and thyme

Place all ingredients into a crockpot and turn on low for 6 hours or high for 4 hours. If more liquid is needed, add just a little.

FALAFEL SANDWICH

12 ounces cooked
  garbanzo beans
1 medium onion, chopped
¼ cup toasted sesame seeds
2 tablespoons parsley

1 teaspoon corainder
1 teaspoon sea salt
  dash chili powder, optional
½ teaspoon cayenne powder

This is called the "Taco from Morocco." You may leave out the hot pepper if you like. Blend the garbanzo beans or place them in a food processor. Add the rest of the ingredients. Place a spoonful or two in pocket bread (pita bread) and top with cheese. You can warm these sandwiches in an oven until the cheese melts and then top with alfalfa sprouts.

FALAFEL TACO

Make exactly as Falafel Sandwich. Place mixture into a taco shell. Cover with warm spaghetti sauce. Sprinkle with grated cheese, chopped lettuce, diced tomatoes, and diced green peppers.

FALAFEL SPREAD

Make exactly as Falafel Sandwich. Add ½ cup Hain Safflower mayonnaise or homemade mayonnaise. Mix together and spread on sandwich or serve on a lettuce leaf as part of your supper.

HUMMUS

½ pound cooked
  garbanzo beans
½ cup Tahini

½ teaspoon sea salt
¼ teaspoon garlic powder
1 teaspoon parsley

Blend all of the above and use as a spread for sandwiches.

KIDNEY BEAN SALAD

3 cups cooked kidney beans
4 boiled eggs, chopped
1 medium onion, chopped

1 teaspoon sea salt
1 stalk celery, chopped
  mayonnaise to moisten

Mix all the ingredients and use just enough mayonnaise to moisten salad.

REFRIED BEANS

3 cups cooks kidney beans or
  pinto beans
1 medium onion, chopped
1 garlic clove, minced

1 teaspoon sea salt
½ teaspoon cayenne pepper
  dash chili powder

Even though these beans are not going to be "refried," it will still give the same idea. Actually "Refritoes" means well fried, not refried. After all the ingredients are together, mash with a potato masher until well blended. Then use in taco shells. It can be heated in a double boiler and cheese added.

BEETS—Have potassium and are high on the list in helping to fight cancer.

Better eaten—Raw or cooked. There are more vitamins and minerals when eaten raw.

Prepare—Wash thoroughly and cut off tops within one inch of the beet. The tops can be steamed and eaten like other greens.

Cook—Boil in water 35 to 45 minutes. Slip off skins when finished cooking. Slice and add butter, if desired.

Steam—6 to 8 minutes.

Ways to use—They can be cut up raw or cooked and put into salads.

BROCCOLI—Has Vitamin A, calcium and potassium. The leaves have more vitamins than the broccoli itself.

Better eaten—Raw is great, but steam it if you like.

Prepare—Wash carefully. Cut about one inch off bottom. Slice lengthwise to get about all the same size pieces. Keep the leaves and steam them also.

Steam—6 to 8 minutes. It should be a little crunchy, not mushy.

Ways to use—Broccoli can be used raw for dips. Just use the tops for dipping. Or cut the tops off for salads. Cheese can be placed on warm broccoli for added taste.

BRUSSEL'S SPROUTS—It has Vitamin A and C, and potassium.

Better eaten—Raw is very good, steam if you desire. There are slightly more vitamins and minerals when eaten raw.

Prepare—Wash thoroughly and remove discolored leaves.

Steam—12 to 14 minutes.

Ways to use—Just plain eating.

CABBAGE—There are several varieties of cabbage—green, savoy, red, Chinese and celery cabbage. It has some Vitamin A and C in it.

Better eaten—Raw

Prepare—Just wash thoroughly and take off the outer leaves.

Steam—10 to 15 minutes

Ways to use—Raw with salads, Cole slaw, in Chinese cooking, soups, sauerkraut, and steamed with potatoes.

COLE SLAW

4 cups shredded cabbage
1 shredded carrot
2 tablespoons apple
   cider vinegar

1 teaspoon sea salt
2 tablespoons parsley
   mayonnaise to moisten

Mix all ingredients and then add mayonnaise to moisten.

CABBAGE AND POTATOES

6 medium potatoes, cut up
1 medium onion, chopped
½ head of green cabbage,
   cut up

2 stalks of celery, chopped
2 carrots, sliced
1 teaspoon sea salt

Place all ingredients in the steamer and steam for approximately 20 minutes.

CABBAGE SALAD

2 cups shredded cabbage
1 stalk clery, chopped
1 banana, sliced

15 or so grapes, halved
¼ cup walnut pieces
   yogurt or mayonnaise to
   moisten

Mix all of the above. If yogurt is used to moisten, add 1 teaspoon honey. Just use enough yogurt or mayonnaise to moisten.

CARROTS—They have the highest Vitamin A content of any vegetable. There are 11,000 International Units of Vitamin A per 100 grams of carrots.

Better eaten Raw

   Prepare—Scrub thoroughly with a vegetable brush. Cut off top and bottoms.

   Steam—6 to 8 minutes when sliced.

Ways to use—Almost all vegetables can be combined with carrots. They can be added to all soups. When grated, they can be used in spaghetti sauce to thicken it. They can be used in tossed salads, cole slaw, and carrot salads.

SESAME CARROTS

Steam 6 medium carrots, sliced. Brown 2 tablespoons sesame seeds in a skillet—no oil. When carrots have finished cooking, top with small amount of butter and sesame seeds.

CARROT SALAD

4 medium carrots, shredded	pineapple chunks (fresh)
1 tablespoon unsweetened	mayonnaise
coconut	nuts
raisins	

Make this salad as small or as large as you like. Add raisins and nuts to your liking. Just put enough mayonnaise in it to moisten the salad.

CAULIFLOWER—It has Vitamin C and potassium.

Better eaten—Raw, there are more vitamins and minerals when raw.

Prepare—Rinse and cut bottom leaves off. For eating raw, cut small florets. For steaming, cut and use all but hard center core.

Steam—12 to 15 minutes

Ways to use—Raw in tossed salads, or with dips. Serve steamed with butter.

CAULIFLOWER POTATO SALAD

1 head cauliflower, steamed	1 grated carrot
½ medium onion, chopped	2 tablespoons parsley
4 boiled eggs, chopped	1 stalk celery, chopped
1 teaspoon sea salt	1 tablespoon apple cider vinegar
	mayonnaise to moisten

This "fake" potato salad will really fool people. Many times, no one has guessed that this was actually cauliflower instead of potatoes. Just mash the cauliflower with a potato masher. Add all the ingredients as you would for potato salad. Then add enough mayonnaise to moisten. Sprinkle the top with paprika and serve as potato salad.

CELERY—Has potassium and some Vitamin A.

Better eaten—Raw and eat the leaves also.

Prepare—Scrub with a vegetable brush.
Steam—8 to 10 minutes

Ways to use—Use in tossed salads, all other salads, soups, casseroles, and chop suey.

CELERIAC—Also known as Celery root.

Better eaten—Raw or steamed
Prepare—Scrub
Steam—8 to 10 minutes

Ways to use—Use as you would celery.

CHINESE PEA PODS—These are a delicacy and sometimes hard to find fresh. They are readily available frozen.

Better eaten—Raw, or slightly cooked
　　Prepare—Wash
　　　　Steam—6 to 8 minutes
Ways to use—It is used in Chop Suey.

CORN—This is high in Vitamin A and has some potassium, along with phosphorus.

Better eaten—Raw — don't faint, but corn is delicious raw, but you can steam it if you like.
　　Prepare—Remove husks, wash and remove corn silks
Ways to use—In soups, casseroles, in succotash with lima beans.

CORN CASSEROLE

6 ears corn, scraped	¾ cup corn meal
2 eggs	½ teaspoon garlic
¼ cup green pepper, chopped	a few pimentos
¼ cup grated Romano cheese	grated cheddar (top)

Mix all the ingredients except the cheddar. Place in buttered casserole dish and top with grated cheddar. Bake 20 to 30 minutes at 350 degrees.

CUCUMBER—Have some Vitamin A and potassium.

Better eaten—Raw
　　Prepare—Wash thoroughly. If waxed on the outside, peel cucumber.
Ways to use—Use raw in tossed salads, other salads and Chop Suey.

EGGPLANT—There isn't too much vitamin or mineral content in eggplant, but it does have fiber.

Better eaten—Cooked or baked.
　　Prepare—Peel skin or prepare with skin according to recipe.
　　　Steam—6 to 9 minutes
Ways to use—Casseroles and with other vegetables.

EGGPLANT CASSEROLE

1 large eggplant,
  peeled, sliced
2 zucchini squash, sliced
1 large onion, sliced
½ pound mushrooms, sliced
1 pound cheddar
  cheese, grated

1 green pepper, chopped
  parsley
  oregano
  garlic powder
  sea salt
1 bottle tomato juice

This mouth watering dish will always bring people back for seconds. They will not realize that there is eggplant in this. If you need more vegetables to fill up your 9"x13" glass baking dish, just slice summer squash. Make layers of eggplant, onions, and mushrooms. Lightly sprinkle the parsley, oregano, garlic and sea salt. Pour tomato juice over this layer. Now, grate the cheese (any natural hard cheese will be fine) and sprinkle that on top of the tomato juice. Next, make a layer of zucchini, onions, mushrooms and pepper. Lightly sprinkle the herbs over this layer. Pour more juice and sprinkle more cheese. Make 2 or 3 layers. Make sure you have enough cheese for the top. If you run out of juice, put a little water in the bottle to get all of it out or use some spaghetti sauce with a little water. Try to get all layers moistened good, but be careful because the vegetables tend to shrink and the juice bubbles over. Try to keep the level of liquid about one inch from the top. Bake about 45 minutes in an oven 350 degrees.

If you want this casserole to be a protein balanced meal, add ½ cup uncooked bulgar.

STUFFED EGGPLANT

1 eggplant, medium
2 tablespoons green onions,
  minced
2 tablespoons green
  bell pepper
10 mushrooms, sliced

¼ teaspoon sea salt
¼ cup whole wheat flour
¼ cup yogurt
¼ cup butter
½ cup grated cheese

Cut eggplant in half lengthwise. Scoop out eggplant leaving some eggplant near the skin. Cut the scooped out eggplant in small pieces. Saute the eggplant, onions, pepper, salt, mushrooms in butter. Remove from heat and stir in yogurt. Spoon into eggplant shell and top with cheese. If you have too much cheese, mix some into eggplant mixture. Bake at 350 degrees for 45 minutes.

BAKED EGGPLANT

1 egg, beaten	sea salt
3 crusts whole wheat bread	parsley
½ cup bran	oregano
1 large eggplant, ¼" slices	thyme
	¼ pound grated cheese

You may peel the eggplant or leave the peeling on. If you leave on the peeling, sprinkle sea salt over the eggplant and let it sit for about 10 minutes. Then rinse the salt off the eggplant slices and pat dry. This helps the peeling be a little more edible. Then dip the eggplant into the beaten egg. Mix the crumbs and bran with a dash of salt, parsley, oregano and thyme. Dip the eggplant into the crumb mixture and arrange in bottom of buttered casserole. Sprinkle grated cheese over the top. You can make several layers, if you desire. Bake uncovered at 350 degrees for 45 minutes.

GREENS—All the greens are very high in Vitamin A.

Better eaten—Raw. They have more Vitamin A content when eaten raw as compared to steamed. Whenever they are cooked, oxylic acid is formed. This is why it is much better to eat them raw.

Prepare—Wash very thoroughly and it even helps to soak them.

Steam—6 to 8 minutes

Ways to use—Use them raw mixed into a tossed salad. Or cook them with onions and potatoes.

Amaranth—This is high in protein

Beet tops—Mild flavored

Chicory—Mild flavored

Collards—Mild flavored

Dandelion—This has 14,000 International Units of Vitamin A per 100 grams

Escarole—Mild flavored

Mustard—Strong flavored

Spinach—Mild flavored, use it in salads and no one knows it is there. It is high in iron and Vitamin A.

Swiss Chard—Strong flavored

Turnip—Strong flavored

JICAMA—Is a delicious root that tastes sweet.

Better eaten—Raw

Prepare—Peel

Ways to use—Slice for salads and use in Chop Suey.

KOHLRABI—This has some potassium

Better eaten—Raw

Prepare—Wash, peel, slice or dice

Ways to use—Cook as a vegetable dish or use in salads, raw.

LEEKS—These are like onions.

Better eaten—Raw

Prepare—Trim off to within two inches of white bulb. Take off outside layer of bulb. Wash.

Steam—6 to 8 minutes

Ways to use—Use raw in salads, make a side dish of steamed leeks and sprinkle with cheese or butter.

LENTILS—Have potassium and magnesium in them. Besides the regular type of lentil, there is an orange colored variety.

Better eaten—cooked

Prepare—Rinse thoroughly and pick out stones and dirt.

Cook—As you would beans, but the cooking time will be shorter.

Ways to use—Use with beans in soups, rice dishes, and salads.

LENTILS OVER BROWN RICE

2 cups lentils	1 garlic clove, minced
1 medium onion, chopped	1 teaspoon sea salt
2 tablespoons parsley	

Boil one quart of water, drop in lentils and all the rest of the ingredients. While lentils are cooking on medium heat, fix brown rice. Rinse 1½ cups brown rice. Bring 4 cups water to a boil with ½ teaspoon sea salt. Add rice and allow water to return to a boil. Then reduce heat to low, cover and cook for about 40 minutes. Lentils should be finished cooking in about 30 minutes. Serve lentils over rice with salad and green vegetable. You will have a protein balanced meal.

LENTIL SALAD

1¾ cups lentils
5 cups water
½ teaspoon sea salt
½ medium onion, chopped

2 tablespoons parsley
1 garlic clove, minced
¼ teaspoon dried thyme
2 tablespoons apple
  cider vinegar

mayonnaise to moisten

Bring water to a boil, drop in the lentils, cover, and turn down the heat to low. Cook for about 30 minutes until tender. Take off heat, add remaining ingredients, cover and place in refrigerator for at least one hour before serving.

LETTUCE—It has Vitamin A and potassium in it.

Better eaten—Raw

    Prepare—Wash thoroughly, break into pieces

Ways to use—Salad

        Bibb—Small leaf

        Boston—Small leaf

    Brown leaf—Very tender with the edges brown or red color.

        Endive—Can either be curly or the Belgian variety.

        Escarole—Leaf lettuce with wide flat stem

        Iceberg—Probably the most popular lettuce called head lettuce.

        Leaf—Green large leaves

        Romaine—Long leaf lettuce used in Caesar salads

    Watercress—square stalk with small round leaves with sharper taste, and it grows in water

MUSHROOM—Are low in calories and have Vitamin D and potassium.

Better eaten—Raw

    Prepare—Wash thoroughly and trim off stem. (They are grown in horse manure.) Slice parallel to stem.

    Steam—14 to 16 minutes

Ways to use—They can be used in almost any dish, with all vegetables. They can be placed in salads, raw. You can make mushroom gravy.

MUSHROOM GRAVY

2 cups water
3 tablespoons arrowroot flour

½ pound mushrooms
¼ cup water
¼ cup tamari sauce

Place arrowroot in ¼ cup water and mix so that all the lumps are gone. If you don't have arrowroot, use whole wheat flour. In a small sauce pan heat up 2 cups water and tamari sauce. Add the arrowroot mixture. Stir until thickened. Add the mushrooms and cook a little longer. This can be used over baked potatoes, or "Burgers" made with Bulgar, called BOB BURGERS.

MUSHROOM/LENTIL SOUP

8 cups water
1 cup chicken stock or
   vegetable seasoning
½ cup lentils
½ cup split peas
1 cup millet
½ cup sliced mushrooms
1 teaspoon parsley

2 tomatoes, cut up
1 carrot, sliced
½ cup onion, chopped
¼ cup green pepper
2 stalks celery, chopped
½ teaspoon garlic powder
   or clove
½ teaspoon dill seed
½ teaspoon sweet basil
½ teaspoon sea salt

Place all ingredients in a crock pot and turn on low. Cook for 6 hours or high for 4 hours. You can cook this on the stove about 2 to 3 hours and it should be tender.

OKRA—Has Vitamin A and potassium.

Better eaten—Raw, but steam if you like

   Prepare—Wash and remove ends. Try to find small pods if eating raw.

   Steam—8 to 10 minutes

Ways to use—Eat them raw—you are in for a surprise. They actually taste better to some people raw rather than cooked. Use them with other vegetables, casseroles, or soups.

OKRA CASSEROLE

1 pound okra, sliced	10 mushrooms, sliced
1 medium onion, sliced	¼ cup green pepper
1 garlic clove, minced	1 tomato, cut up
1 cup tomato juice	¼ cup bulgar or bran
1 teaspoon oregano	Cheese

Mix together in a casserole all of the above except the cheese. Sprinkle grated cheese on the top. Bake at 350 degrees for 50 to 60 minutes.

ONIONS—Green onions have Vitamin A and potassium. The dried onions have less Vitamin A than the green ones.

Better eaten—Raw

    Prepare—Peel the bulbs or if a green onion, cut up green to eat.

    Steam—6 to 8 minutes

Ways to use—In just about everything

Small white—Whole dried for cooking

    Yellow—Seasoning

      Red—Seasoning

    Spanish—Sweet for salads

    Bermuda—Sweet for salads

      Italian—Sweet for salads

    Scallion—Any of three varieties of onion—the shallot, the leek, or the green onion with a long, thick stem and almost bulbless root.

PARSNIPS—Have potassium and are similar in appearance to a carrot, except they are white.

Better eaten—Raw or steamed

Prepare—Wash and scrape. Leave whole or cut into slices

Ways to use—Eat with butter, or sprinkle with parsley, bake them or mash them.

PEAS—Split peas are higher in Vitamin A content than green peas.

Better eaten—Fresh peas are better eaten raw from the pods. Then eat the pods, taking off the inside "skin."

Prepare—Fresh peas have to be removed from the pod. Split peas are rinsed and cooked like other dried vegetables until tender.

Steam—Fresh 6 to 8 minutes, frozen 10 to 12 minutes.

Ways to use—As a vegetable dish, in soups, and casseroles.

PEPPERS—Have Vitamin C and A. Red peppers have the edge over the green ones in vitamin content. Green bell and red bell peppers are sweet. There are others which are very hot, like Jalapeno, chili peppers and cayenne.

Better eaten—Raw

Prepare—Wash thoroughly and cut up.

Steam—6 to 9 minutes

Ways to use—Use raw in salads, add to casseroles, and use in Mexican dishes.

POTATOES—Have a lot of potassium. There are either the new potatoes, which are small red ones or the white potatoes. Some are Idaho bakers.

Better eaten—Cooked, raw or baked

Prepare—Wash and scrub, leave peelings on

Steam—14 to 18 minutes

Ways to use—Can be eaten raw, used in salads. Baked or boiled with the skins on. Broiled as french fries. Mashed or added to soup. When you mash the potatoes, don't throw away the water — use it instead of milk for liquid.

POTATO SALAD

3 pounds potatoes (9 medium)
1 whole onion, chopped
2 stalks celery, sliced
2 teaspoons sea salt
4 boiled eggs, sliced
1 carrot, grated

¼ cup olives
2 tablespoons parsley
¼ cup apple cider vinegar
¼ cup water
1 cup mayonnaise
paprika

Boil potatoes in peelings until tender. You can keep the peelings on or remove them. Chop the potatoes into small bitesize chunks. Add the other ingredients, reserving several slices of eggs for the top along with a few olives and a sprig of parsley. Add mayonnaise to potato salad. If you want a juicy potato salad, add the ¼ cup water. Place garnishes on top and sprinkle paprika.

POTATO SOUP

1½ quarts liquid
   (water or whey)
10 medium potatoes, diced
   and 2 grated
1 carrot, grated
2 tablespoons butter

1 clove garlic
1 medium onion, chopped
¼ teaspoon basil
2 teaspoons sea salt, try less
   and then add if needed

Clean and scrub potatoes, dice them, leaving the peelings on. Grate 2 of them and the carrot. This will add thickness to the soup. Add all the ingredients and cook. If you make cottage cheese and don't know what to do with the whey, try this recipe. The potato soup will taste like it has yogurt in it. Even though it is unusual, it would be very nourishing.

OVEN FRENCH FRIES OR FRIED POTATOES

Use baked potatoes or cooked potatoes
Safflower oil
Sea salt

Cut potatoes into strips or if making fried potatoes, slice. Toss strips or French fries lightly in a bowl with a few drops of safflower oil and sea salt. Place on a baking sheet under the broiler until golden brown. Turn often. For Oven Fried potatoes, slice onions and lightly drizzle safflower oil over sliced potatoes and onions. Broil, turning often.

POTATO DUMPLINGS

2 quarts boiling water

2 pounds potatoes

2 eggs

2 teaspoons sea salt

2 teaspoons baking powder

1 cup whole wheat flour

1 tablespoon parsley

pinch of nutmeg

Cook potatoes until tender, cool and grate. Combine potatoes with eggs, salt, nutmeg and flour. Work to form dough. Pinch off enough to make a two inch ball. Drop dumplings into 2 quarts boiling water one at a time. Allow water to return to boil and cook about 15 minutes.

PUMPKIN—It is high in Vitamin A.

Better eaten—Cooked or baked

> Prepare—Take pumpkin out of the shell and cook. Take out any strings. Seeds can be toasted and are delicious and loaded with nutrients.

Ways to use—In a casserole and in pies. Pie recipe under DESSERTS

RADISHES—Have Vitamin C and potassium. Can either be red or white

Better eaten—Raw

> Prepare—Cut stems and wash

Ways to use—In salads

RUTABAGAS—Have Vitamin A and potassium. Raw ones are slightly higher in vitamin content.

Better eaten—Raw

> Prepare—Scrub, cut off roots and tops, peel if waxed and cut into slices or cubes.

Ways to use—Raw in salads or cook as a vegetable, topped with butter as you would potatoes. They have a strong taste and some people add a potato to the pot.

SALSIFY—Also called the oyster plant

Better eaten—steamed

> Prepare—Scrub and scrape and then drop into 1 quart of water which has had 1 tablespoon vinegar placed in it. Drain and slice.

> Cook—Boil in salted water 20 to 30 minutes.

Ways to use—Just as a vegetable dish.

SPINACH—Check under GREENS

SQUASH—It has Vitamin A and potassium

Better eaten—Raw

    Prepare—Scrub and wash thoroughly, leaving skins on.

    Steam—8 to 10 minutes

Ways to use—Some squash is good raw in salads, others should be baked.

    Crookneck—Summer squash, good raw in salads, yellow in color

Straight neck—Summer squash, good raw in salads, yellow in color

    Cymling—white squash. It can be baked or cooked.

    Pattypan—white squash. It can be baked or cooked.

    Scalloped—white squash. It can be baked or cooked.

    Italian—Very large squash with a tough skin. The seeds are rather hard to eat. The vegetable men call this "Italian squash," but I am sure it has a more proper name. It is a summer squash.

    Cocozelle—Dark green, striped lighter green and is a summer squash.

    Chayote—Light green.

    Zucchini—Dark green and only needs to be steamed 5 to 7 minutes. This squash is very good raw in salads.

    Acorn—Winter squash which should be baked. You can bake it in a glass pan filled with a little water for about 1 hour at 350 degrees.

    Butternut—Winter squash that you can bake like an acorn squash.

    Hubbard—Winter squash that you can bake like an acorn squash.

    Spaghetti—Winter squash used in place of spaghetti.

    Turban—Winter squash, some are ornamental, can be red.

BAKED YELLOW SQUASH

4 crookneck yellow squash	2 tablespoons butter
1 medium onion, sliced	parsley

Scrub squash, but do not peel. Cut off stems and blossom end and then cut lengthwise. Melt butter and pour in small glass baking dish. Spread onion slices in dish and lay squash over them. Sprinkle with parsley, and put ½ inch water in the dish and bake at 350 degrees for about 20 minutes.

SUMMER SQUASH CASSEROLE

2 eggs
½ cup bran
1 teaspoon sea salt
1 teaspoon Tamari sauce
2 tablespoons parsley

3 cups summer squash, blended
¼ pounds mushrooms, sliced
1 medium onion, chopped
¼ cup green pepper, chopped
1½ teaspoon sweet basil grated cheddar cheese

Blend 3 cups of squash. This could be crookneck and zucchini or your choice. Mix all of the above ingredients, except the cheese. Butter a casserole dish either 8"x10" or 6½"x10". Pour in the casserole and top with grated cheese. Bake at 350 degrees for 30 minutes.

SWEET POTATOES—They are in the morning glory family.

Better eaten—Cooked, baked or raw

Prepare—Wash and scrub potatoes, do not peel.

Cook—In boiling water with a little salt for 30 to 35 minutes.

Ways to use—Eat as a vegetable with butter or make into a casserole.

TOMATOES—Have Vitamin A and some C.

Better eaten—Raw

Prepare—Just wash and cut out end where stem is.

Steam—4 to 5 minutes

Ways to use—With almost any vegetable, in soups, casseroles and tossed salads.

GAZPACHO

Tomatoes blended to equal-
2 cups puree
1 large cucumber
1 large onion
1 green bell pepper

⅓ cup ripe olives, reserve for top
¼ cup olive oil
¼ cup apple cider vingar
1 chili pepper
1 teaspoon garlic or 1 clove
1 teaspoon vegetable seasoning

Blend tomatoes to equal 2 cups liquid. Reserve a small portion of onion, pepper, cucumber, and tomato to garnish soup. Blend up all the rest of the vegetables along with oil, vinegar, chili pepper and garlic. Chill at least 3 hours. Serve cold with garnishes on top.

TURNIPS—Have a little potassium in them. They are called yellow turnips.

Better eaten—Raw

>   Prepare—Cut off tops (you can eat those, too), wash and pare thinly.

>   Steam—18 to 20 minutes

Ways to use—Raw in salads, cooked with butter or mashed

WATER CHESTNUTS—It is an aquatic plant native to China. It can be used in Chop Suey.

Better eaten—Raw

>   Prepare—Wash, peel, slice.

Ways to use—In Chop Suey, on salads.

YAMS—Are high in potassium and have a high starch content.

Better eaten—Cooked or baked

>   Prepare—Wash and scrub yams, do not peel.

>   Cook—In boiling water with a little salt for 30 to 35 minutes.

Ways to use—Eat as a vegetable with butter or make into a casserole

YAM SOUFFLE

2 cups mashed yams	$\frac{1}{4}$ cup honey
2 eggs	$\frac{1}{2}$ cup nuts
$\frac{1}{2}$ teaspoon salt	$\frac{1}{2}$ teaspoon cinnamon

Mix all ingredients together and put in casserole dish. Bake 30 to 35 minutes at 350 degrees.

VEGETABLE STEW

1½ pounds fresh green beans
6 potatoes, scrubbed
1 medium onion, chopped
1 cup fresh lima beans
  or frozen

2 stalks celery, sliced
2 carrots, sliced
1 garlic clove or 1 teaspoon
1 cup fresh black eyed peas
  or frozen

Quarter the scrubbed potatoes and cook in 1 quart of water. When they are about half cooked, add the green beans and other vegetables. Cook at least 30 minutes until all vegetables are tender, but not overcooked.

CHOP SUEY

1 whole onion, chopped
¼ cup green peppers, chopped
2 stalks celery, sliced
½ cup cucumber pieces,
  optional
½ cup water chestnuts or
  Jerusalem artichokes, sliced
¼ cup squash, chopped

¼ cup peas
½ pound mushrooms
  pea pods, optional
  mung bean sprouts
3 tablespoons Tamari sauce
2 tablespoons arrowroot
  flour

Saute onions, peppers, celery, mushrooms, squash (yellow or zucchini), cucumber, water chestnuts, and peas in a small amount of liquid. You can use chicken stock, apple juice or water. When the vegetables appear glassy, add 2 to 3 tablespoons of Tamari sauce. Do not add salt because Tamari tastes salty. Thicken ½ cup water with 2 tablespoons arrowroot flour. Pour thickened water into vegetables and stir. Now add water to bring the level up to just about cover the vegetables. If you don't want that much liquid, pour in a little. Continue stirring until it is mixed well. Add the pea pods and bean sprouts. Vegetables should be crunchy, not over cooked.

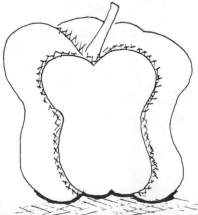

STEP-BY-STEP CHECK LIST FOR FRUITS AND VEGETABLES

Yes

1. I have served fruit 3 times instead of desserts. ——
2. I now make sure the fruit bowl is always filled. ——
3. I have sent fruit in my child's lunch instead of a gooey dessert. ——
4. I sent dried fruit with my child for a snack in his lunch. ——
5. I tried a mixture of dried fruit and nuts and the children liked it. ——
6. I served a dish of nuts and dried fruits for guests and they ate it. ——
7. I tried steaming a vegetable for supper. ——
8. I stopped buying canned vegetables. ——
9. I am buying almost all fresh vegetables. ——
10. I tried making a "new" vegetable for my family. ——
11. I had beans and rice for supper instead of meat. ——
12. I served one new raw vegetable to my family and they ate it. (If they didn't like it, try another one.) ——
13. We are eating raw vegetables every day. ——
14. My family is eating more vegetables than before. ——

CHAPTER 4

SALADS AND SPROUTS

SALAD GUIDE

Greens	Raw Vegetables	Protein	Garnishes
Lettuce:	Artichokes-Jerusalem	Hard cheese,	Alfalfa
Bibb	Avocado	strips	sprouts
Boston	Asparagus tips	Boiled eggs	Bean sprouts
Brown leaf	Beets	Cooked beans,	Black olives
Endive	Broccoli	½ cup	Green olives
Escarole	Brussels sprouts	Sunflower	Onion rings
Iceberg	Carrots	seeds, ¼ cup	Gr. bell
(head)	Cauliflower	Sesame seeds	pepper ring
Leaf	Celery	¼ cup	Red bell
Romaine	Celeriac	Almonds ½ c.	pepper ring
Watercress	Corn	Walnuts ½ c.	Beet strips
Green Tops:	Chinese Pea Pods	Cashews ½ c.	Cherry toms.
Amaranth	Cucumbers		Sliced mush-
Beet tops	Garlic		rooms
Chicory	Jicama		Eggs,
Collards	Kohlrabi		quartered
Dandelion	Leeks		Carrot curls
Kale	Mushrooms		Grated
Mustard gr.	Okra		Romano
Spinach	Onions		Cheese
Swiss Chard	Peas		
Turnip gr.	Peppers		
Cabbage:	Potatoes		
Green cabbage	Radishes		
Savoy cabbage	Rutabagas		
Red cabbage	Scallions		
Chinese cabbage	Yel. straightneck squash		
	Yellow crookneck squash		
	Zucchini squash		
	Tomatoes		
	Water chestnuts		

SALADS

Fresh green salads are important in cancer prevention. There are so many combinations, that the list is endless. With a little imagination, even a dull cook can whip up a gorgeous salad. Someone has said that making a salad is a work of art and takes talent. But for those without talent, there is one sure way of getting the job done—and that is copy. Yes, just copy what you have seen others do. One valuable convenience that I have found for all salad lovers is an electric food processor. This enables a person to cut down on kitchen time without cutting out needed nutrition. Whereas before, it took close to an hour to create a gorgeous mouth-watering salad with all the cut up vegetables, it now takes about 20 minutes from start to finish. Many times I would elimate certain vegetables because it would just be another thing to get out and cut up. One night, I felt rather industrious and worked very hard on a salad that had 28 different raw vegetables in it. But don't copy that! It definitely had too many different vogotabloo. I would havo boon bottor off ocrving a oalad with the uoual raw vegetables and a separate plate of one or two raw vegetables.

Salads are appealing to eat when they are beautiful. I am convinced that if you make food gorgeous to look at, people will want to eat it. Don't just sprinkle your garnishes on the top of the salad—arrange them in an order. Make a design with the food. For children, make funny faces on their salads, using olives for eyes, onions for eyebrows, carrot stick for a mouth and a cherry tomato for a nose. Eating a salad can be fun for children.

Salad recipes are a waste of time. You are only going to make a salad with ingredients you have on hand. With the SALAD GUIDE you can use whatever is available at your house, be creative, and yet have a nutritious salad. Some type of salad is served at our house every day of the week. With this guide you may branch into some new areas you have never thought about. Try to mix the greens so that one flavor isn't predominant. This way, if someone detests spinach, they will eat it with the lettuce and never know they had it. Break up the greens into bitesize pieces and be sure to wash thoroughly. Don't let the salad dressing "soak" on the salad. Pour it over when serving. If you have other protein in your meal, you can eliminate putting protein in the salad. However, if you are relying on the salad for protein, then double up on the amounts given. When choosing raw vegetables for your salad, go easy on the new ones to your family. It would be better for a child to say, "I just ate a piece of raw broccoli," then to have him sit and look discouragingly at his salad with 14 pieces of raw broccoli in it! In other words, introduce raw vegetables to them slowly a little at a time.

Instead of a tossed salad, or cabbage salad, why not try a raw vegetable tray with a dip. Arrange many of your family's favorites along with several new raw vegetables. Now would be a good time to try raw okra. Leave the stem on so that they can hold the stem, dip it, and bite off right at the stem. Be sure to use very small tender okra. The larger ones are tougher. Make it a game. Everyone has to try the new vegetable. Brussels Sprouts are also fun to dip. Among our favorite raw vegetables are cauliflower, broccoli, mushrooms, okra, and celery stuffed with cream cheese.

GREEK SALAD

Large bowl of	6 Greek peppers
assorted greens	15 black ripe olives or
10 mushrooms, sliced	Greek olives
4 tomatoes, quartered	onion rings
5 scallions, sliced	green pepper rings
	Feta cheese

Cauliflower potato salad or regular potato salad, pages 58 and 67
Italian dressing, page 81

In the bottom of your salad bowl, place a large amount of potato salad or cauliflower potato sald. Don't be afraid to use the cauliflower recipe. It is delicious and I have served it to company without them knowing what it was. They loved this Greek Salad.

Next, place your greens in the bowl with all the vegetables, except the garnishes.

Garnish with the onion rings, green pepper rings, Greek peppers, black olives, a few tomatoes. Sprinkle Feta cheese over the salad and alfalfa sprouts.

Pour Italian Dressing over the entire salad.

You may also choose other raw vegetables such as cucumbers, radishes, jicama, carrots, celery, and squash to include in your salad.

BASIC TOSSED SALAD

Large bowl of
assorted greens
4 radishes, sliced
1 carrot, sliced
1 stalk celery, sliced
2 tomatoes, quartered
2 scallions, sliced
½ cucumber, sliced

Garnishes:
¼ cup green olives
3 onion rings
3 green pepper rings
10 black olives
5 cherry tomatoes
alfalfa sprouts
5 mushrooms, sliced

This salad can be made as large or as small as you desire. This will give you a start on making a gourmet salad. If you want to introduce people to raw foods, I would suggest using this salad and adding raw broccoli, or raw cauliflower.

LETTUCE PLATE SALAD

On a small plate, make a bed of lettuce

ADD:
Sliced tomatoes
Red radishes
Avocado
Carrot sticks
Celery sticks
Scallions
Bell Pepper slivers
Cottage cheese
Cucumber slices
Mushroom slices
Jerusalem artichoke slices

TOP:
olives
Alfalfa sprouts
Sesame seeds

ZUCCHINI SALAD

cabbage, shredded
onion, chopped
celery, chopped
zucchini, sliced

Cook for 1 minute:
¼ cup honey
¼ cup apple cider vinegar
1 teaspoon celery seed
½ teaspoon sea salt

Use as much or as little of the vegetables as desired. All the vegetables should be raw. Cook the seasoning just one minute and mix with the cabbage, onions, celery, and zucchini.

SALAD DRESSINGS

MAYONNAISE

1 egg
½ teaspoon sea salt
¼ teaspoon cayenne pepper
2 tablespoons honey

4 teaspoons apple
  cider vinegar
7 teaspoons lemon juice
1¼ cups safflower oil

Put all ingredients into a blender, except the safflower oil. When they are well blended, slowly, very slowly add the safflower oil. Soon the mixture will become thickened. If you want it to be sweet, add a little honey.

CAESAR DRESSING

¼ cup olive oil
¼ cup water
1 oz. apple cider vinegar

½ teaspoon sea salt
½ teaspoon garlic powder
½ teaspoon onion powder
2 tablespoons parsley

Shake well in a bottle. Pour over Romaine lettuce. Sprinkle with grated Romano cheese.

YOGURT SALAD DRESSING

1 cup homemade mayonnaise
½ cup plain yogurt
2 scallions, cut up
2 tablespoons lemon juice
½ teaspoon garlic powder

1 clove garlic, minced
½ teaspoon sea salt
½ teaspoon oregano
1 teaspoon parsley
½ teaspoon onion powder

Blend all of the ingredients.

WILTED SPINACH DRESSING

¼ cup apple cider vinegar
¼ cup safflower oil
1 medium onion, chopped

½ cup water
½ teaspoon paprika
2 boiled eggs, chopped

Heat all of the above ingredients, except the egg. Sprinkle over washed spinach. Add chopped eggs.

BLUE CHEESE DIP

½ cup plain yogurt
½ teaspoon garlic

½ cup mayonnaise
¼ pound blue cheese

Mix ingredients and crumble the blue cheese into dressing. Sometimes you can find expensive blue cheese dressing that does not contain preservatives or sugar. A tablespoon or two of this can be substituted for the blue cheese.

ITALIAN DRESSING

¼ teaspoon oregano
¼ teaspoon garlic
¼ teaspoon thyme
¼ teaspoon marjoram
¼ teaspoon tarragon
½ teaspoon sweet basil

¼ cup water
½ cup olive oil
¼ cup apple cider vinegar
1 tablespoon chopped chives
½ teaspoon sea salt

Mix all the ingredients and shake well in a bottle.

HOW TO GROW YOUR OWN SPROUTS

Sprouts are so nutritious because they are the "germ" of life itself. They are really the *beginning*. Sprouts have much better and higher protein value than the food which grows from the seeds. The increased lysine and tryptophan help the protein content of sprouts. Also the vitamin values increase in sprouting. Vitamin C content is five times higher, Vitamin B increases, along with E and K in sprouting. Sprouts are just plain good eating. A person can sprout almost any seed. Here is a suggested list.

Seeds	Whole Grains	Whole Dried Beans & Peas
Alfalfa	Wheat	Mung
Unhulled sesame	Barley	Garbanzo
Unhulled sunflower	Triticale	Green peas
Radish	Oats	Kidney
	Rye	Lentils
	Corn	Lima
		Pinto
		Red
		Soy

Perhaps the most popular sprout is the bean sprout used for years by the Chinese. Coming up fast in the race of sprouts is alfalfa. Alfalfa is known as the "Father of all Foods." It is a member of the bean family and is a clover-like plant. It was first cultivated in ancient Persia, then Greece, Spain and later brought to America. For many years, it was by-passed and now scientists find that alfalfa leaves contain a higher percentage of trace minerals than any other plant. It also contains 8 essential enzymes, potassium, magnesium, iron, calcium, phosphorus, chlorine, silicon, sulphur, sodium, Vitamins A, D, E, K, B-6, and U. It has many healing qualities such as bringing down high blood pressure, lowering cholesterol levels, and loosening stiffened joints from arthritis. These tender nutty morsels are a favorite on salads, soups, and hot vegetables. In fact, many restaurants are using them.

You do not need anything special to grow your sprouts. Just use a clean, wide mouth, quart-size glass jar. You can use a double layer of nylon net, or nylon stocking (clean, please), or cheesecloth for the top held securely by a rubber band.

To start alfalfa sprouts, place about 1 tablespoon alfalfa seeds in the bottom of the jar. Cover the seeds with water and allow them to sit for about four hours. Pour off this water. You may use it to water your plants, as it is loaded with enzymes. Then rinse the seeds pouring off the water. Turn the jar sideways, so that the sprouts will spread out a little and leave the jar on your counter top or in the cupboard. Rinse with water twice a day, morning and night, pouring off the water. After about 5 or 6 days, you will notice the sprouts are about an inch to two inches long. The green, or chlorophyll, is from the light. Your sprouts are ready to eat and should be refrigerated, with the original lid.

Mung bean sprouts are sprouted exactly the same way with the exception of the time allowed to sit. Leave the mung beans sitting in water all night. Rinse in the morning and place in the cupboard. Rinse a few times during the day. Mung beans take between 3 to 4 days to sprout. When they are one to one and a half inches long, they are ready to eat and should be refrigerated.

There are several other methods for sprouting. One is to keep the seeds on a damp paper towel and sprinkle them with water throughout the day. Plastic sprouters can be used also. The glass jar method is the easiest and least expensive and even works for people who have a "brown thumb."

Garbanzo beans take about three to four days to sprout and are between ¾" to 1" long. They are better cooked. Lentils take 2 to 3 days and are the same length as the seed. Rye and wheat take 2 days to sprout and are the same length as the seeds. Soybeans take 3 to 4 days to sprout and are ½" to ¾" long. Watch out that a mold doesn't come on the soybeans. Rinse thoroughly and drain. Sprouts can be used in almost any salad, sandwich, casserole, vegetable dish, breads and soups.

STEP-BY-STEP CHECK LIST FOR SALADS AND SPROUTS

Yes

1. I slipped raw spinach into the salad and no one noticed it.   _____
2. I made a gigantic salad with several new raw vegetables for dinner.   _____
3. My family enjoyed "dipping" raw vegetables   _____
4. I grew my own alfalfa sprouts.   _____
5. I grew my own bean sprouts.   _____
6. We are eating sprouts just about every day now.   _____
7. We now eat a salad every day.   _____
8. I now use more than one kind of lettuce in my salad.   _____
9. I added a "new" raw vegetable to my salad and everyone ate it.   —
10. We tried having just a salad meal like Greek Salad for supper.   ___

CHAPTER 5

HERBS AND SPICES

HERBS AND SPICES

Herbs and spices seemed to be used interchangeably to season foods. Spices are from the roots, bark, berries, and fruits of plants. Herbs are the leaves of shrubs. Herbs are usually grown in the North Temperate Zone and can be used for medicinal treatments. Many pharmaceutical companies are now using herbs as medicine, even though herbs have been used for centuries to cure ailments. In fact, herbal remedies are used extensively the world over.

HOW TO USE 38 HERBS AND SPICES

ALLSPICE—This is not a combination of spices, but actually a plant which is similar to cinnamon and cloves. It is used with meats, desserts, rice, Brussels sprouts, carrots, corn, squash, eggplant, potato, tomato sauce, fish, chicken.

ANISE—is similar to fennel in that it has a licorice taste. It is a seed used in fish dishes, soups, and oriental dishes. It is mentioned in the Bible in Matthew 23:23.

BASIL—is called sweet basil. It is excellent with tomato, avocados, squash, greenbeans, cauliflower, corn, cucumbers, garbanzo beans, vegetable and fish soup, eggs, greens, rice, chicken, fish, and beef.

BAY LEAF—Psalm 37:35 refers to a Bay Tree with aromatic leaves. They are used in bean soups and vegetable soups, stews, chicken, fish, and beef. Use in flour and cupboards to keep out bugs.

CARAWAY—seeds are used in breads and cheeses, stews, chicken, rice.

CARDAMON—is similar to ginger and used with soups, some fruits, lamb stews, mushrooms, squashes, and pumpkin.

CAYENNE—is red pepper used sparingly with seafood, beans, soups, eggs, cabbage, mayonnaise, green beans, peas, collards and mustard greens, corn, lima and butter beans, okra, mushrooms, onions, spinach, blackeyed peas, zucchini, and turnips.

CELERY SEEDS—can be used in dips, fish, stuffed eggs, rice, potatoes, scrambled eggs, green peas, onions, zucchini, beets, and carrots.

CHERVIL—is similar to the Biblical myrrh and is fragrant. It is used on eggs, peas, and fish.

CHILI PEPPERS AND POWDER—used in Mexican food such as tacos and casseroles. Use very sparingly until taste is right.

CHIVES—part of the onion family with small slender green leaves. Use to flavor eggs, salads, dressings, fish, and soup.

CINNAMON—used in the Bible in Exodus 30:23 and Proverbs 7:17. It is a bark which can be boiled for tea and ground for a spice. It is used with fruit, desserts, eggplant, parsnips, sweet potatoes, squash, pumpkin, beets, and apple cider drinks.

CLOVES—can be used with chicken, soups, apple cider drinks, pumpkin, relishes, beets, carrots, onions, squash, and sweet potatoes.

CORIANDER—is used in Bible times and mentioned in Exodus 16:31 and Numbers 11:7. It adds to chicken dishes, greens, casseroles, garbanzo beans, and mushrooms.

CUMMIN—is mentioned in the Bible in Isaiah 28:25,27 and Matthew 23:23. It is used in soups, vegetables, beans, eggplant, corn, avocado, rice and potatoes.

CURRY—is used in India and is a mixture of strong spices such as pepper, ginger, garlic and coriander. Curry has been used with lamb and rice.

DILL SEED AND WEED—used in pickling, relishes, fish, salads, eggs, casseroles, cucumbers, beets, cabbage, green beans, celery, carrots, tomatoes and onions.

FENNEL—is similar to anise and has a licorice taste. It is used in casseroles, rice dishes, potatoes, fish, artichokes, cabbage, and eggplant.

GARLIC—is mentioned in the Bible in Numbers 11:5. It is a member of the onion family, but with much more taste and odor. It can be used with beans, soups, casseroles, meats, salads, dressings, cucumbers, and vegetables.

GINGER—is a spicy flavored root from tropical Asia. It is used in Asian cooking, casseroles, beets, desserts, Brussels sprouts, onions, green beans, green peas, parsnips, sweet potatoes, pumpkin, and fruit.

LEMON BALM—is used where a lemon flavor is desired. It is also made into a tea.

MACE—fruit of the nutmeg tree which can be eaten with bean, pea, lentil soups, fish, chicken, broccoli, cabbage, and eggs.

MAJORAM—is used in soups, dressing, stuffing, scrambled and stuffed eggs, fish, potatoes, rice, chicken, lamb, beef, casseroles, beets, Brussels sprouts, carrots, corn, split peas, lima or butter beans, parsnips, mushrooms, sweet potatoes, and turnips.

MINT—is mentioned in the Bible in Matthew 23:23. It is a cooling fragrance used for tea, jellies, meat, green peas, sweet potatoes, squash, fruit salads, beets, and cucumbers.

MUSTARD—is mentioned throughout the Bible illustrating how a great tree can grow from a tiny seed. Matthew 13:31-32, Luke 13:19 and Mark 4:32 make reference to mustard. It is used in mayonnaise, beans, onions, potato salad, spinach, zucchini, stuffed eggs, and cucumber.

NUTMEG—is used in desserts, eggs, fish, chicken, beans, carrots, cauliflower, corn, onions, applesauce, fruits, parsnips, sweet potatoes, squash, beet greens, and Brussels sprouts.

OREGANO— is part of the mint family. It is used in spicy cooking such as spaghetti, pizza, tomato dishes, bean soups, fish, chicken, mushrooms, onions, cabbage, green peppers, broccoli, garbanzo beans, and cucumbers.

PAPRIKA—is the fruit of the capisicum pepper plant. It is mild and can be used with eggs, potato salad, chicken, kidney beans, lima beans, onions, cabbage, cucumbers and garbanzo beans.

PARSLEY—a vitamin rich plant with leaves that are used in almost any dish, except desserts. It has Vitamins A and C, potassium and calcium.

PEPPER—is from India and East Indies. Black pepper is ground from the dried berries, white pepper is from the dried seeds with the coating removed, cayenne is from the red pepper. Since it is hot, use sparingly. It can be used with any vegatable, casserole or meat dish. Pepper is not recommended for cancer control patients. Black pepper is NOT used in a cancer prevention diet.

POPPY SEEDS—can be used with potatoes, broccoli, Brussels sprouts, cabbage, carrots, lima beans, parsnips, sweet potatoes, and rice.

ROSEMARY—is a shrub of the mint family. It can be used in soups, eggs, split peas, eggplant, green peas, zucchini, beans, casseroles, cauliflower, corn, and chicken.

SAGE—is from the mint family and aids digestion. It is used in stuffing, chicken dishes, squash, fish, eggplant, tomatoes or summer squash.

SAVORY—has a slight peppery taste and is from the mint family. It is used in bean dishes, white potatoes, zucchini, and cauliflower.

SORREL—sour tasting leaves used in salads and some vegetables.

TARRAGON—is a plant of the aster family. It's called the "King" of herbs by some people. It is used in salads, dressings, fish, stuffed eggs, chicken soup, greens, green beans, mushrooms, parsnips, white potatoes, squash, tomatoes, cauliflower and asparagus.

THYME—is part of the mint family and is helpful in digestion. It is used in meat dishes, soups, eggs, casseroles, lentils, green beans, okra, bell peppers, squash, asparagus, beet greens, cauliflower and carrots.

TUMERIC—is a bitter root that is used for yellow dye.

STEP-BY-STEP CHECK LIST FOR HERBS AND SPICES

Yes

1. I have tried to include more herbs and spices in my cooking.   ——

2. I have started to purchase one new herb each week.   ——

3. I have begun to use one new herb or spice each week.   ——

CHAPTER 6

PROTEIN

PROTEIN

The Bible gives us some instruction on what to do about meats. In the first 2,000 years, man ate plants and herbs. After the flood, man was permitted to eat animals, as recorded in Genesis 9:2-3. Strict warning was given not to eat the blood. Instruction was given in Exodus 12:8 as to eating the passover lamb. Fish are mentioned several times in regard to food; once, when the Children of Israel remembered their life in Egypt, given in Numbers 11:5, and when Lord Jesus ate fish and honeycomb in Luke 24:42. Matthew 14:17-19 gives the miraculous account of the Lord Jesus feeding 5,000 people on 5 loaves and 2 fishes. Meat was not eaten each day, but on festive occasions. One example is when the fattened calf was killed for the celebration of the returning Prodigal Son. Leviticus 11:4 gives warning not to eat any animal which is cloven footed or cheweth his cud.

In our modern age it would be better if we would all turn to being a vegetarian, or a lacto-vegetarian, which is a person who eats vegatables, cheese and eggs. Some day we may be forced to do this, and so it would be good to start cutting down now.

AMERICAN PROTEIN INTAKE COMPARED TO THE WORLD'S

Our American society is so animal protein conscious that they eat approximately 65 grams of protein each day. And yet, the rest of the world survives on about 15 grams per day. Realistic studies have shown that the protein need is actually 25 to 35 grams. What a drastic difference. We seem to be blind to some of the pitfalls of high consumption of meat. In areas where more beef is consumed, there is a higher rate of colon cancer. According to the Beef Industry Council, Americans consumed 120.5 (carcass weight) pounds of beef in 1978. When cooked it comes to 41.7 pounds of beef eaten per person a year, or 1.8 ounces eaten each day. This does not include fish, poultry, pork and other meats.

EATING LARGE AMOUNTS OF MEAT IS JUST A HABIT

Since we are creatures of habit, eating so much meat has just been passed on because of such an affluent society. Frances Moore Lappe made an amazing discovery in 1968, according to her book, Diet of a Small Planet. She discovered that protein fed to animals, which could have been eaten by humans, would come close to the whole world's protein deficit. This is an amazing fact. We are feeding good grains to animals just to fatten them in order for selfish Americans to satisfy their fleshly desires, when the rest of the world could be fed with that same amount of grain. It makes a person stop to think when they dive into all those steaks, chickens and hamburgers each day. I have found that a little meat can go a long way. Once you begin eating vegetable protein, your body doesn't crave meats.

You feel satisfied because your digestive system is not working so long and hard to digest the meat.

Another reason to turn people "off" of meat is the fact that our American meat is so contaminated. No other country in the world wants our meat—they know what's in it. And yet, we go blindly on gorging ourselves with meat—morning, noon and night and even for midnight snacks. Pesticide residue is higher in meat, fish and poultry than any other products we eat. One of the chemicals, DES or Diethylstilbesterol is injected into the cattle to fatten them up sometime before they are slaughtered. DES is a known carcinogen, yet the Department of Agriculture claims that this saves the American consumers about 3ᶜ per pound. Big deal. If you eat beef, try to buy from a rancher who doesn't use DES. Chickens have been tested and contain antiobiotics, arsenic, and adrenalin, and sodium iodacetate.

Hot dogs, containing 30% meat and 70% trash, are required to have nitrates or nitrites in them; or they can't be called a hot dog. Besides this cancer causing chemical, they have dyes. They used to contain Red Dye No. 2 and some probably still do.

Pork has trichinosis, a dangerous parasite. Each week Americans consume about 180,000 pounds of this infected pork. The trichinosis-free pork is shipped out of the country. Fish cannot escape the pollution of the world. Methyl-mercury levels have been found in many of the coastal fish. Fish from Greenland and cleaner waters do not carry damaging poison like other fish. If you are going to eat fish, use white flesh fish and try to find less polluted ones from clean water.

Besides being contaminated, meat can slow down the healing of the body. This is one of the reasons people on a cancer control diet should eliminate meat. If meat is really desired, it could be eaten once a week. Whenever I tell people that meat is eaten about once a week at our house, people gasp in horror. They tell me that their husband would never stand for that. After all he was a "meat and potato man!" I simply smile and think back to the pounds and pounds of meat my husband consumed before he realized how damaging excess protein was to the body. Now, his body never craves meat and he eats very little. What a switch. Once a person becomes informed and realizes that his life is at stake, a change should come. Eating a lot of meat is just a habit. Anyone can break a habit if he really sets his mind to it.

Eating more protein than necessary can cause problems within the body. In breaking down excess protein, a toxic build-up in the tissues causes uric acid to accumulate, intestinal troubles and too much acid. Excessive meat harms the body in yet another way. As meat is broken down, it forms "ammonia." Tests have shown this to be another carcinogen. Fasting can rid the body of harmful poisons, but it should be done under a doctor's care. Not everyone can fast; and hypoglycemic persons are just one example.

DO YOU NEED A LOT OF PROTEIN?

Many people ask the question, "How can I be sure I am giving my family enough protein, if I don't serve meat?" The best way to answer that is to look at the statistics. You are probably getting twice as much protein right now than your body actually needs. And besides, meat is not the best source of protein according to the protein scale. Even the quality or usability of the meat protein is less than eggs or milk. So, a person can see that animal protein is not all what it is "cracked up" to be.

Another question people ask is "Isn't it boring just eating vegetables?" I tell them, aren't there basically only five different meats that most people eat? What could be more boring than only 5 meats as compared to the 97 vegetables discussed in this book. There are many interesting vegetable combinations, casseroles, and ways to fix them. Also all the nuts, grains and fruits add a lot of variety.

Some people are concerned about the cost. In comparing grocery tabs with other average families, I can't see where our bill is any higher than theirs. Since we have eliminated just about all doctor bills and kept meat to a minimum, there is extra money to put into fresh foods.

Beans are a good source of protein to substitute in place of meat. The cost is so much cheaper than meat. If you were to figure the cost of the actual protein in beans, it would be about $3.00 per pound. Egg protein would be $6.00 a pound and the protein in round steak would cost $12.00 a pound. There might come a day when all of us are happy to eat beans as a source of protein if prices keep soaring. Another good point about bean and grain protein is that it contains fiber. Meat does not contain fiber, thus becoming stagnant within the body.

GETTING THE RIGHT PROTEIN COMBINATION

Proteins have certain amino acids. Some authorities feel that there are 8 essential amino acids and others feel that there are 10. Whichever is right makes little difference. What does matter is that you get all eight to make a protein balanced meal. The following chart will help in matching grains, milk or cheese, and vegetables to gain a complete protein. Egg is called a perfect protein and needs no other ingredient to compliment it. Milk and cheese can be used interchangeably. If you begin planning your meal around these complete protein combinations, and add vegetables, then you can feel assured that your family is getting a complete protein. In many cases it will be better than a meat protein. Cancer control people should try to eat their protein at lunch.

PROTEIN COMBINATIONS CHART

Although each line compared may not be of equal protein value, each ingredient on a line will make a complete protein if combined. For instance, beans and rice used in a meal will make a complete protein.

Beans	and	Rice
Beans	and	Wheat
Beans	and	Cheese
Beans	and	Corn
Beans	and	Sesame Seeds
Potatoes	and	Milk
Potatoes	and	Cheese
Rice	and	Milk
Rice	and	Cheese
Rice	and	Sesame Seeds
Rice	and	Wheat and Seeds or Nuts
Sesame Seeds	and	Milk or Cheese
Wheat	and	Cheese

CHICKEN RECIPES FOR MEAT EATING FRIENDS

I don't advocate eating a lot of chicken, and especially frozen, fried or pre-packaged chicken. The only reason chicken recipes are included in this book is for my friends who are trying to get their family "onto" natural foods. The white meat of chicken and turkey are easier to digest than beef. For this reason, chicken, and turkey are suggested to replace excess beef consumption, if meat is desired. And then only fresh chicken is used, especially from a farmer who feeds his chickens properly. Our family eats chicken once a week with an occasional fish dinner during the week. They are completely satisfied with vegetable meals.

BAKED CHICKEN AND BROWN RICE

1 whole fresh frying chicken	¼ pound mushrooms, sliced
1 stalk celery, sliced	½ onion, chopped
1 carrot, sliced	1 clove garlic, chopped
1 cup brown rice, rinsed	½ cup yellow squash
4 cups water	chopped
Parsley	¼ cup green bell pepper
½ teaspoon coriander	½ cup zucchini, chopped
	sea salt

Take all skin off chicken and place in large roaster. Place all vegetables, brown rice, water and seasonings around chicken. Be sure to sprinkle seasoning on the chicken. You may use any vegetables, such as broccoli, cauliflower, zucchini squash, or whatever you have on hand. Bake covered at 350 degrees for 1½ hours or until rice is soft.

SHAKE IN A BAG CHICKEN

1 cup bran	½ teaspoon garlic powder
¼ teaspoon sea salt	½ teaspoon onion powder
2 tablespoons parsley	1 tablespoon dried onions

Place all the above ingredients in a large bag. Remove skin from chicken pieces and shake in the bag. Place in a glass baking dish, uncovered and bake at 350 degrees for approximately 1 hour and 15 minutes, or until chicken is done. Some smaller chickens are finished within one hour.

CHICKEN TETRAZZINI

chicken pieces	1 garlic, minced
8 ounces spaghetti*	1 onion, chopped
Bottle of spaghetti sauce	¼ cup green bell peppers
10 mushrooms	2 cups tomato juice
½ cup zucchini squash, sliced	sea salt to taste
	cheese, optional

Skin pieces of chicken while spaghetti is cooking. Place cooked spaghetti into large glass baking dish (13"x9"). Sprinkle in onions, zucchini squash, mushrooms, garlic, peppers and enough tomato juice to moisten all of it. Place chicken pieces on top of spaghetti and spoon spaghetti sauce over each piece of chicken. Your dish may dry out a little, so put enough tomato juice to make it juicy, but be careful it doesn't run over the sides. If you like, place a little grated cheese on the top of each piece of chicken. Bake uncovered for 1½ hours at 350 degrees.

*The spaghetti used in this recipe is not the kind from the grocery store, but artichocke spaghetti which is white and tastes like regular spaghetti. Or, you can use whole wheat spaghetti which is brown in color. Use 1 or 2 teaspoons of safflower oil when cooking pastas, so that noodles will not stick to one another.

VARIATIONS: Use Vegie-macaroni in place of spaghetti. This is macaroni made from vegetables and can be purchased at some health food stores. Use whole wheat noodles in place of spaghetti or use artichoke noodles.

CHICKEN CHOP SUEY

¼ cooked chicken
1 whole onion, chopped
¼ cup green peppers, chopped
2 stalks celery, sliced
½ cup cucumber pieces, optional
½ cup water chestnuts or Jerusalem artichokes, sliced

¼ cup squash, chopped
¼ cup peas
½ pound mushrooms
    pea pods, optional
    mung bean sprouts
3 tablespoons Tamari sauce
2 tablespoons arrowroot flour

Saute onions, peppers, celery, mushrooms, squash (yellow or zucchini), cucumber, water chestnuts, and peas in a small amount of liquid. You can use chicken stock, apple juice or water. When the vegetables appear glassy, add 2 to 3 tablespoons of Tamari sauce. Do not add salt because Tamari tastes salty. Thicken ½ cup water with 2 tablespoons arrowroot flour. Pour thickened water into vegetables and stir. Now add water to bring the level up to just about cover the vegetables. If you don't want that much liquid, pour in a little. Continue stirring until it is mixed well. Add the pea pods, bean sprouts and chicken. Vegetables should be crunchy, not over cooked. Serve over brown rice.

CHICKEN AND NOODLES

Cooked chicken pieces
8 ounces noodles
1 onion, chopped
½ pound mushrooms, sliced
  sea salt to taste

½ cup peas or
  green vegetable
2 tablespoons parsley
1 teaspoon sweet basil
2 cups chicken broth,
  approximately
  gated cheese, optional

Cook noodles with 1 teaspoon safflower oil. You may use artichoke noodles, which are white or whole wheat noodles, or spinach noodles. Place noodles in glass baking dish (13"x9"). Mix all ingredients with noodles. Chicken pieces have already been previously cooked. Make sure you have enough liquid. Sprinkle cheese on top. Bake at 350 degrees for about 20 to 30 minutes.

CHICKEN CASSEROLE

Saute in 2 tablespoons safflower oil until vegetables appear "glassy"

½ cup scallions
1 small green pepper, sliced
½ cup carrots, cut thin
½ cup zucchini squash, cut thin
½ cup celery, sliced
½ cup water chestnuts or
  Jerusalem artichockes
½ teaspoon fresh ginger, minced
  or ½ teaspoon ground ginger
2 garlic cloves, minced
1 cup fresh mushrooms, sliced

Add:

2 tablespoons arrowroot powder mixed with
½ cup chicken stock
2 tablespoons Tamari sauce

Combine:

2 cups cooked brown rice
2 cups cooked chicken, cut up
½ cup pea pods
½ cup cashews

Saute the first list of ingredients in oil, add the second list to thicken vegetables and combine the last list to finish this superb casserole, made right on the top of the stove.

ROSALIND'S BAKED FISH

Saute in 2 tablespoons olive oil for 5 minutes:

2 medium onions, chopped
2 garlic cloves, minced
2 tablespoons parsley
3 tomatoes, peeled and chopped

Prepare 2 pounds fish filet with:

3 tablespoons lemon juice
   Sea salt

Garnish with:

1 sliced tomato
1 sliced lemon
1 teaspoon oregano
¼ cup water

While vegetables are cooking, pour lemon juice and sprinkle sea salt over fish. Pour sauted vegetables over fish. Place slices of tomato and lemon over fish. Add ¼ cup water. Bake uncovered for 30 to 45 minutes, depending upon how thick the fish, at 350 degrees.

BAKED FISH

Fresh fish filets
1 tomato, cut up
2 stalks celery, sliced

1 onion, chopped
½ green pepper, cut up
1 teaspoon lemon juice
tomato juice

Soak fish in goat's milk for at least two hours. Just pour enough milk to cover fish. This will take away much of that "fishy" taste that makes people turn their noses up at baked fish. Pour the milk off when ready to bake. Place all cut up vegetables on top of fish and pour tomato juice so that it does not cover fish, but covers the bottom of dish. Bake at 350 degrees for 30 minutes or until fish is flaky.

FISH CHOWDER

fish filets
2 quarts of liquid
2 onions, chopped
4 potatoes, cubed
1 garlic, minced

4 cups any vegetables
chopped
(zucchini, yellow squash,
peas, carrots, lima beans)
sea salt, to taste

Place all ingredients in large pot to cook, except fish. If you want the fish to remain in chunks, place in pot when vegetables are half cooked. If you want the fish to disappear (flounder will), then cook it the entire time. Cook until vegetables are soft about 45 minutes to 1 hour.

My children do not care for fish, but they love this chowder. The whole secret is that they cannot see any fish in it when they eat it.

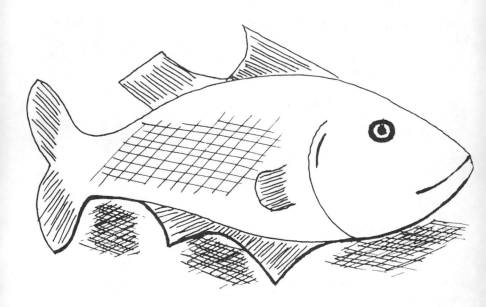

MAIN DISH RECIPES
BEAN LOAF

2 cups cooked kidney beans
1 cup soaked bulgar to make
  3 cups
2 cups grated cheese, reserve
1 cup for top

1 whole onion, chopped
¼ cup green pepper, chopped
½ teaspoon sea salt

Blend kidney beans or mash them. Add rest of the ingredients. Use one cup of cheese in the bean mixture. Reserve one cup for the top. Bake in a glass baking dish in loaf form at 350 degrees for 20 to 30 minutes.

SKILLET DINNER

Saute in ¼ cup butter:

½ cup scallions, chopped
½ large green pepper, chopped
1 cup celery, chopped
10 mushrooms, sliced

Add:

3 cups cooked brown rice
½ cup sunflower seeds
½ cup sliced almonds
2 teaspoons coriander

Top:

2 ripe tomatoes, cut in wedges
½ pound cheddar cheese, grated

After sauteing vegetables, add the second group of ingredients. Then top with tomatoes and cheese. Just heat long enough to melt the cheese.

BLACK BEANS OVER RICE

2 cups black beans or
  12 ounces in
1 quart of boiling water with
  2 Bay leaves

1 garlic clove, minced
2 tablespoons parsley
2 teaspoons sea salt
1 medium onion

Drop beans into boiling water with bay leaves and turn off. Cover and let sit for 1 hour. After hour, add rest of ingredients and cook on medium heat until tender. While beans are cooking, make rice. Rinse 1½ cups brown rice. Bring 4 cups water to a boil with ½ teaspoon sea salt. Add rice and allow water to return to a boil. Then reduce heat to low, cover and cook for about 40 minutes. Serve black beans over rice with salad and green vegetable.

One of the best recipes for company is the following Pizza Recipe. This will go over good with people who have never had natural food and who never want to try any.

PIZZA CRUST

1 package or tablespoon yeast	1 teaspoon sea salt
1 cup warm water	2 tablespoons safflower oil
2 teaspoons baking powder	2 tablespoons honey
	2½ cups whole wheat flour

Melt the yeast in the warm water. Then add the baking powder, salt, oil, honey, and flour. Dough should be thick. Dust the pizza pan with cornmeal or butter lightly. This will be enough dough to make two 12" round pizza sheets, or 1 round sheet and 1 cookie sheet (10"x13"). Flatten the dough into the pans with your fingers. You can make the dough very thin or thick, depending upon the way your family likes it. Then bake the crust at 425 degrees for about 10 minutes or until the crust is golden brown. Take out of oven. Now you are ready to decorate your pizza.

PIZZA

1 crust
Spaghetti sauce—spoon over entire crust

STEP 1:	STEP 2:
Sprinkle:	Decorate:
Sea salt	Chopped onions
Parsley	chopped green peppers
Garlic powder	sliced mushrooms
Onion powder	STEP 3:
Oregano	Cheese:
	Grated romano cheese
	Grated white cheddar, 1 pound
	Grated provolone, 1 pound

First give a generous layer of spaghetti sauce, which does not contain sugar or preservatives. Then sprinkle the list of ingredients. Go lightly at first until you have tasted the pizza and know what your family likes. Next decorate with the vegetables your family likes. Top with the three cheeses used by one of the best professional pizza makers I ever knew. Now bake your masterpiece at 425 degrees until the cheese melts about 5 minutes. Cut your pizza with a scissors. (It's easier than a knife or pizza roller.)

FREEZING PIZZA

1. You can freeze the crust on the cookie sheet, pizza pan or glass cookie sheet. Once frozen, remove crust and wrap for continued freezing. This saves a lot of time when unexpected guests stop in.

2. You can make the entire pizza, including the 1st baking, decorate and freeze. Once it has frozen, you may remove it from the pan and wrap for continued freezing.

Once we set up a "little pizza shop" in our home and made 11 pizzas in one day. All of them went into the freezer and were used throughout the next couple of months for company, emergencies, and quick suppers.

MEATLESS SPAGHETTI SAUCE

½ cups lentils, cooked
2 cups red kidney beans
2 cups tomatoes, chopped
2 whole onions, chopped
¼ cup green pepper, chopped
½ teaspoon sea salt
1 cup sliced mushrooms
2 stalks celery with tops, chopped
2 teaspoons oregano
¼ teaspoon cayenne

1 teaspoon onion powder
1 teaspoon garlic powder
1 tablespoon chives
1 tablespoon parsley
½ cup tomato juice
2 tablespoons olive oil
water—just as little as possible so that spaghetti is thick

You may boil a quart of water and drop in lentils and kidney beans with 2 bay leaves. Then turn off the heat. Allow the beans to sit 1 hour. Pour off the excess water and reserve it for later. Put in all the rest of the ingredients and simmer. Add the water you reserved earlier, if needed. Pour over spaghetti noodles.

LASAGNE

Cook: 8 ounces of whole wheat lasagne noodles with 2 teaspoons safflower oil in water

Get ready: MEATLESS SPAGHETTI SAUCE or purchased spaghetti sauce
3 cups ricotta cheese or cottage cheese
1 pound grated cheddar or provolone cheese

Butter a baking dish 13"x9". Begin layers of meatless spaghetti sauce, lasagna noodles, cottage cheese, and grated cheese. Repeat layers ending with cheese. Bake uncovered for 45 minutes at 350 degrees.

BOB BURGERS

3 cup cooked bulgar
10 mushrooms, sliced
1 egg
1 whole onion, chopped
¼ cup green bell pepper

½ teaspoon garlic
2 tablespoons Tamari Sauce
1 tablespoon Tarragon
3 tablespoons w.w. flour
2 cups grated cheese

Mix all the ingredients with the bulgar. Form into patties. It should make about 11 patties. Place under broiler for about 5 minutes or until tops are golden brown.

EGGPLANT CASSEROLE WITH BULGAR

1 large eggplant, peeled
  & sliced
2 zucchini squash, sliced
1 large onion, sliced
½ pound mushrooms, sliced
½ cup uncooked bulgar

1 green pepper, chopped
1 bottle tomato juice
  oregano
  garlic powder
  Sea salt
1 pound cheddar cheese
  grated

Using a 9"x13" glass baking dish, just make layers with all the ingredients, including the tomato juice and cheese. Sprinkle a light amount of each vegetable, bulgar, cheese, seasonings, and juice. Be sure to end up with cheese on the top. Read the Eggplant Casserole Recipe under egg plant in VEGETABLES, if you want further information. Bake this casserole at 350 degrees for 45 minutes to 1 hour.

TACOS

Corn Taco shells

Filling:

Use "Meatless Spaghetti sauce and add a dash of chili pepper and ¼ teaspoon more cayenne pepper until it tastes "hot" enough to suit your family; ground cummin should be added.

Or

2 cups cooked kidney beans, mashed
    cayenne pepper and chili powder to suit your taste
    small amount of tomato juice to make the beans juicy or
2 cup up tomatoes

Start with filling in bottom of taco shell, sprinkle with grated cheese, chopped lettuce and tomato. Let each person make his own for added fun.

SEEDS

The Bible is quite definite on man's eating seeds. In Genesis 1:29, we read, "And God said, Behold, I have given you every herb bearing *seed*, which is upon the face of all the earth, and every tree, in which is the fruit of a tree yielding seed; to you it shall be for meat." The most fascinating part of this Scripture is that seeds can be used in place of meat. In fact, sunflower seeds contain more protein than steak, but they must be added to other foods because they are an incomplete protein.

Seeds are the "Beginning of Life," consequently they contain so many valuable vitamins and minerals. After all, future life is stored in these precious little gems. The following are a few of the seeds which have not been discussed previously.

SEED LIST

CHIA—These seeds are from the mint family and are native to California, Mexico and South America. They have been used for hundreds of years in soups and beverages. The early California missionaries used them for medicinal purposes. They are good for cancer patients.

FLAX—This plant is valuable for its stem, which is made into linen. It is mentioned several times in the Bible, Exodus 9:31, Joshua 2:6, Isaiah 19:9, Proverbs 31:13 and Matthew 12:20 (Also Isaiah 42:3 which is the same as Matthew 12:20). The stalks were spread on flat roofs and dried. The fine fibers were woven like wool. The seeds are used to make linseed oil. Flax seeds can be used in bread making.

PUMPKIN—These seeds are more popular than other vegetable seeds. They are high in phosphorus and protein. It is best to eat them raw. Add them to salads, casseroles, sandwiches, etc.

SESAME—This is one of about twenty species of an herb family, native to southern Africa and eastern Asia. Sesame has been cultivated for a very long time and is valuable for the seeds. The unhulled seeds contain more vitamins. They should be ground for better absorption by the body. Sesame oil is extracted from the seeds. In ancient times, sesame was used for food, medicine and other important uses. They are high in calcium, phosphorus, protein, potassium, and magnesium. Sesame seeds can be used in cookies, casseroles, made into milk and with vegetables. Tahini is sesame seeds ground into a sesame butter.

SUNFLOWER—This is an herb native to North America. The plant is used for fodder, but the seeds are eaten raw. The valuable sunflower oil is extracted from the seeds. Sunflower seeds are high in phosphorus and potassium. The sunflower seed is 98% digestible and has more protein ounce for ounce than steak. Seeds contain twelve minerals, seventeen vitamins, and ten amino acids. It is high in unsaturated fatty acids. They can be added to salads, casseroles, cookies and cakes.

APRICOT SEED OR PITS—This is the small bitter nut encased in a hard shell inside the apricot fruit. This seed along with apple seeds and peach seeds contain nitrilosides which are important in fighting cancer. The Hunza people in the Himalayan Mountains thrive on apricot seeds and consider them to be very valuable. An interesting note about these people is that there has never been one case of cancer among them, as long as they stay on their natural diet. A few seeds a day can be beneficial along with a natural diet.

NUTS

There are several nuts mentioned in the Bible. In Genesis 43:11, almonds and nuts are given as a gift along with honey, spices, and myrrh. The nuts are considered to be pistachio nuts, native to western Asia. The "garden of nuts" referred to in Song of Solomon 6:11, is a walnut. It is cultivated in Galilee. Almonds are mentioned quite frequently throughout the Bible. There are two varieties, bitter and sweet. They are recorded in Ecclesiastes 11:5, in Exodus 25:33 where the golden candlesticks are carved like almond blossoms, and in Numbers 17:8 when Aaron's rod budded and brought forth almond blossoms. The twig or rod of an almond tree signifies Jehovah's wakefulness as recorded in Jeremiah 1:11, 12. Hazel and chestnuts are mentioned in Genesis 30:37.

Nuts are a good source of protein and contain vitamins, minerals and unsaturated oils. Generally they contain less usuable protein than the seeds and they are higher in calories than other sources of protein. However, don't be discouraged, a small amount of nuts can go a long way in lending protein to a diet.

NUT LIST

ALMOND—originated from countries around the Mediterranean. There are two varieties, bitter or sweet. The tree is part of the rose family. It contains 18.6 grams protein per 100 edible grams. It is high in nitrilosides and unsaturated fatty acids.

BRAZIL—is from a tropical tree. The nuts contain 14.3 grams protein per 100 edible grams.

CASHEW—is a native of tropical climates. These nuts contain 17.2 grams protein per 100 edible grams.

CHESTNUT—is in the beech tree family. It is especially native to China and northern temperate regions. The American chestnut is almost extinct. The nuts are considerably lower in protein than the other nuts with only 2.9 grams per 100 edible grams.

COCONUT—is the nut of the coconut palm, native to tropical climates. The meat around the kernel is dried and can be purchased unsweetened. The kernel itself can be steamed and eaten. The liquid or coconut milk can be consumed. Dried coconut meat has 3.5 grams per 100 edible grams.

FILBERT OR HAZELNUT—is found in Europe, West Asia and North Africa. It has a protein content of 12.6 grams per 100 edible seeds.

HICKORY—is from the walnut family and has several varieties of edible nuts. They are found throughout Europe, Asia, Africa and eastern United States. The most common variety is the pecan.

MACADAMIA OR QUEENSLAND NUT—is native to southern California, Hawaii and Florida. They are very costly per pound.

PEANUT—is not really a nut, but a legume. It is very high in protein —26 grams per 100 edible grams. It is grown in the south.

PECAN—is in the hickory family, growing in the south and eastern part of the United States. It has 9.2 grams per 100 edible grams.

PEKEA—is an edible nut from South America.

PINON or PINYON NUTS—are grown in Mexico and California.

PISTACHIO—is a member of the cashew family, growing in the Mediterranean area. These nuts have approximately 15 to 20 grams protein per 100 edible grams.

SAPUCAIA—is called a paradise nut and is similar to a Brazil nut.

SQUARI OR SUARROW OR SAWARRA—is native to Surinam, South America. The nut is like a Brazil nut, but tastes a little like an almond. They are very hard to get.

WALNUT—is native to North America and southeastern Europe and eastern Asia. The Black walnut has more protein 20.5 grams than the English walnut with 14.8 grams per 100 edible grams.

There are many interesting recipes using nuts and seeds. You can combine any nut or seed with rice to make a delicious casserole. The following is an interesting recipe with a catchy title. The reason this tuna is happy is because he isn't in it! It is hard to convince people that this isn't tuna.

HAPPY TUNA

1 ½ cups almonds, blended
1 ½ cups cashews, blended
2 carrots, blended

¼ cup apple cider vinegar
¼ cup water

Blend a small amount of raw almonds and cashews until the entire 3 cups are blended. Then blend the 2 carrots. Add the vinegar and water to the blended mixture and mix well. This is the basic Happy Tuna. Now, add whatever you desire. Here is a suggested list.

Celery, onions, boiled eggs, and green peppers.

If your mixture gets a little too dry, add more water and it will appear as if you have added mayonnaise. Serve on a lettuce leaf or in a sandwich. Be careful because it is very filling.

WALNUT CASSEROLE

4 cups cooked long grain
  brown rice
1 cup English walnuts, ground
2 eggs
2 tablespoons fresh parsley
2 celery stalks, chopped

½ cup chopped onions
½ teaspoon sea salt
¼ cup chopped green pepper
10 mushrooms, sliced
1 teaspoon coriander
1 garlic, minced
1½ cups to 2 cups
  grated cheese

If you use the basic brown rice recipe, you will yield approximately 3 to 4 cups cooked brown rice. In a buttered large glass baking dish, mix all of the above ingredients well. Mix the cheese in at the same time, reserving some for the top. Bake at 350 degrees for about 30 minutes.

CHEESE

Cheese has been around for many years. In the Old Testament, I Samuel 17:18, David is recorded taking ten cheeses, along with other food, to his brothers in the army of Israel. Cheese is mentioned again in Job 10:10. In Job, the cheese is referred to as curdled cheese better known today as "Cottage Cheese". It is believed that the "butter and milk" Abraham gave to the three men in Genesis 18:8, was actually curds or yogurt. Here again in II Samuel 17:29, scholars feel that the "Cheese of Kine" for David is referring to Yogurt. Butter references are scattered at least 11 times throughout the Bible. However, it was not butter as we know. Milk was placed into a skin and kneaded, then the contents were taken out, heated and put into a goat's skin bottle. In the summertime, the butter was oil and in winter, it was the consistency of honey. However, the cheese or butter references are not clear as to whether the original milk was cow's milk or goat's milk. Some of the cheese references could mean yogurt as well as hard cheese.

Cheese is generally considered the curd of milk which has been coagulated, separated from the whey, and then pressed. The coagulation comes about when rennet, or the extract from the fourth stomach of a calf or sheep, has been added to the milk. It is a good source of protein, Vitamin A, Calcium, and phosphorus. It contains 7 times as much protein as the milk from which it is made.

Natural cheeses are better than processed cheese, because heat is used to make it quickly and air is used to "puff" it up. Also cheese that does not have coloring is better than those with additives and dyes. Some cheese may say "made from raw milk", but all cheese has to be heated at certain temperatures for various lengths of time. Be sure to buy cheese that does not have preservatives. There are over four hundred different names of cheeses in the United States and other countries, but there are probably no more than eighteen different varieties. Cheese can be frozen.

Goat's milk and goat cheese are much easier for the body to digest than cow's milk and cheese. Many times babies will be given goat's milk when nothing else would agree with them. Goat's milk and cheese should definitely be used by cancer control patients, if they desire to use a dairy product. Goat cheddar is another form of goat cheese, but with a distinct flavor. Goat cheeses can be frozen, but cream cheese does not freeze well.

COTTAGE CHEESE

If cottage cheese is desired, allow whole milk to sour and clabber at room temperature for about 3 days and nights. Then heat in the top of a double boiler for 20 minutes on low heat, stirring once in awhile. Strain clabbered milk. The cottage cheese can be lightly salted and if desired, more milk can be added for a creamy texture. The whey, which is the left over liquid, can be used as a nutritious drink. A sharp tasting potato soup can be made from it.

YOGURT

Much has been said about the advantages of acidophilus. Buttermilk and yogurt are good sources of this. Basically, the intestinal flora consists of good and bad bacteria. The good bacteria perform several functions. They help synthesize important vitamins, principally vitamin K, as well as some members of the B-complex vitamins such as riboflavin, niacin, biotin, and folic acid. Yogart contains calcium, protein and some potassium. Another important function of intestinal bacteria is in helping the colon to maintain a proper acid balance essential to good elimination. This is accomplished principally by a type of micro-organism called "lactobacilli" or lactic acid bacteria, which split lactose or milk sugar to form lactic acid. This accounts for the tart taste. Several different strains of lactic acid bacteria are as follows: Lactobacillis Acidophilus, Lactobacillus Bulgaricus, Lactobacillus Caucasicus, Streptococcus Thermophilus, and Plocamo-bacterium Yoghourtii.

Commercial yogurts should be checked to see if the label reads "active cultures." Some yogurts are pasteurized thus destroying the acidophilus. Starters can be purchased to make yogurt or 2 table-spoons from an active cultered plain yogurt can be used.

HOMEMADE YOGURT

Mix 1⅓ cups powdered milk (from the Natural Food Store) with 1 quart of water, either in a blender or in a jar. You may also use 1 quart of goat's milk, if you desire, in place of the powdered milk and water.

Place in a pan on medium heat, stirring occasionally until hot, but do not boil and do not scorch. Allow the milk to cool approximately 1 hour. Now add 2 heaping tablespoons of an active cultured plain yogurt.

Then cover your pan or bowl and place in a nice warm spot for at least 8 hours. A hot garage or a car sitting in the sun is perfect. Or if you don't have any sun, try a wide mouthed thermos bottle, covered and left eight hours. You can also use a glass jar placed in a pan of warm water on an electric stove turned to warm for about 5 hours.

Now remember to save at least 2 tablespoons for your next batch of yogurt.

WAYS TO EAT YOGURT

Eat plain yogurt, sweetened with honey.

Add fruit to yogurt and sweeten with honey, if needed.

Use with mayonnaise for "dips".

Use as a topping on desserts.

Kefir is made from Kefir grains and somewhat like yogurt, but a little sweeter.

It is used in Bulgaria and Russia as part of a daily diet.

Puma is used as a substitute for milk. It is not as sweet as Kefir.

EGGS

Contrary to popular opinion, eggs do not add cholesterol to the blood stream. They are a completely balanced protein. Cholesterol is manufactured by the body. When the cholesterol or tryglycerides are too high, then we know the body is not functioning properly. Usually the diet that a person goes on when the cholesterol is high, is sufficient to bring down the cholesterol count. It is interesting to note that the person usually decreases meat and sugar intake, and eats an all around better diet; which could account for the fact that the cholesterol is reduced. Studies have shown that withdrawing sugar and meat causes the cholesterol to drop.

The white of eggs contain 10% protein while the yolk has 16% protein. Eggs contain almost all nutrients, with the exception of Vitamin C. Fertile eggs are supposed to be better than unfertile.

Eggs should be purchased straight from the chicken farmer. Try to find out what his chickens are eating and get the freshest eggs possible. Grocery store eggs have sometimes been sitting on the shelf for quite awhile.

Cancer control people should limit their use of eggs to two a week.

WESTERN SCRAMBLED EGGS

6 eggs
1 cup water or
  goat's milk
¼ cup green pepper,
  chopped
¼ cup onions, chopped
bean sprouts, optional

2 tablespoons parsley
1 tomato, cut up
10 mushrooms, sliced
⅓ cup any vegetable
½ cup cheddar cheese

Mix eggs well, add liquid and cheese. Pour into skillet over medium heat. Drop in all other ingredients. For the vegetables, you may use zucchini or summer squash, cooked kidney beans, or your preference. Add salt if desired.

EGG SALAD

6 eggs, boiled
  & chopped
2 stalks celery, sliced
¼ cup onion, chopped

¼ cup green pepper
  sliced
¼ teaspoon sea salt
2 tablespoons parsley
  mayonnaise

Mix all of the above ingredients with enough mayonnaise to moisten. Use for sandwiches or serve on a lettuce leaf.

STUFFED EGGS

6 boiled eggs,
  sliced in half
parsley
onion powder, sprinkle
garlic powder, sprinkle

mayonnaise
¼ teaspoon sea salt
paprika

Slice eggs in half, mix yolks together with onion and garlic powder and enough mayonnaise to moisten. Add parsley and salt. Replace yolk in white and sprinkle with paprika.

SANDWICHES

Sandwiches are such a part of the American way of life, that we probably couldn't get along without them. Since we have already discussed bread in an earlier chapter, you should have made the switch at that time to a whole wheat natural grain bread. Or better yet, perhaps you are making your own bread. Whatever the case may be, the following list will give you an idea of sandwich breads:

Purchased whole grain bread without sugar or preservatives

Purchased whole grain bread from a natural food store

Purchased whole wheat rolls from a natural food store

Homemade whole wheat bread and rolls, rye bread & rolls, Pita
   bread or pocket bread, purchased or homemade

Taco shells

Corn Tortillas

Now for the filling! With a little imagination, you can create your own sandwich specialties. Here is our standard cheese sandwich. For those on a cancer control diet, it is recommended that they stay with the Goat cheese.

CHEESE SANDWICH

bread spread with mayonnaise
sliced tomatoes
lettuce leaf

alfalfa sprouts
sliced hard cheese or
goat cheese

VARIATION:

TOASTED CHEESE SANDWICH

Place 2 slices of bread in broiler with cheese on one. Melt cheese and remove. Add lettuce, tomatoes and sprouts.

One of the most delicious sandwiches I have ever eaten is the following. Sometimes you can get it in health minded restaurants. It is so filling, a person can use it for an entire meal, or add a vegetable dish with it. It's terrific with soup.

VEGETARIAN ECSTASY

Bread—spread with thin layer
   of mayonnaise
Sliced raw mushrooms
Sliced cream cheese
Grated zucchini squash

Sliced tomatoes
Lettuce
Sliced cucumbers
Onion, chopped, small amount
Alfalfa sprouts

Make into a "dagwood" sandwich. It's great for a quick supper.

VARIATION: Additional slice of hard cheese.

DIANE'S DELIGHT

1 cooked chicken breast
3 medium cooked potatoes
½ medium onion
1 tablespoon chopped parsley
10 mushrooms, sliced
1 ounce cup green pepper,
   diced

1 stalk celery, chopped
   few green olives
½ teaspoon sea salt
1 carrot, grated (optional)
1 teaspoon garlic powder
   mayonnaise to make
   spread

Blend the potatoes with their peelings on along with the chicken. Mix all the rest of the ingredients with potatoes and chicken. Use just enough mayonnaise to make the mixture spreadable.

Other sandwich fillings are:

EGG SALAD, page 111

FALAFEL SANDWICH, page 55

FALAFEL SPREAD, page 55

HUMMUS, page 55

HAPPY TUNA, page 106 (no tuna in this one)

PEANUT BUTTER & HONEY

REFRIED BEANS, page 55

TACOS, page 102

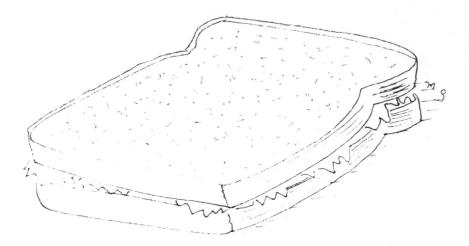

OILS AND FATS

The oil mentioned in the Bible is olive oil. In Proverbs 27:9 and Isaiah 1:6, the Bible refers to the use of ointment, which is olive oil. Then in I Kings 17:16 the Bible records the widow's oil as never running out.

Generally speaking, oils are liquid at room temperature and fats are solid at room temperature.

Saturated fatty acids are found in animal fats. Butter, shortening, and lard are examples.

Unsaturated fatty acids are found in both animal and vegetable fats. Examples are safflower oil, soybean oil, peanut oil, corn oil, cottonseed oil, avocado, sesame oil, walnut oil, sunflower seed oil, and wheat germ oil.

Polyunsaturated fatty acids are in liquid vegetable oils. They have two bonds in their chemical chain such as linolei and linolenic acid.

The encyclopedia describes shortening as plastic materials made wholly from fats and oil. This plastic shortening goes through elaborate processes of stripping, heating, agitating, deodorizing, bleaching, antioxidizing, flavorizing, chilling, and packaging. Margarine is an emulsion of edible plastic fats with some form of milk, emulsifying agents, sodium benzoate, artificial coloring, flavors, and vitamins. Then it is pumped full of hydrogen.

Some of the best oils to use are safflower oil, sunflower seed oil, olive oil, and avocado oil. All but safflower oil are carriers of oxygen and have anti-rancidity components. Safflower oil from the grocery store is probably rancid when you purchase it because of the process used to obtain it. The safflower oil from a natural food store should read "cold pressed." This means that the oil was expelled from the seeds without the use of chemicals. However, according to Dr. Airola most cold-pressed oils are not *really* cold-pressed. He feels that the only oils in the United States that would truly be cold-pressed oils are olive, sesame seed or sunflower seed oils which are purchased from a natural food store.

Cottonseed oil should not be used because all of the cotton has been sprayed with pesticides.

It is better to use oils instead of butter. Usually butter is used in recipes for taste, but with a little experimentation, oils can be used in place of butter. In fact, safflower oil can be used to replace ½ the amount of butter in every recipe in this book.

Lecithin can be used to grease pans for baking, but it is hard to use. Studies have shown that lecithin helps keep down cholesterol.

Heating will change fats and oil. The higher the heat, the more damage is done. Most oils and fats become carcinogenic when frying. It is best to never fry foods.

STEP-BY-STEP CHECK LIST FOR PROTEIN

Yes

1. I fixed one meatless protein balanced meal for my family and they liked it.   _____

2. We are now eating some seeds as snacks and in lunches.   _____

3. We are now eating nuts as snacks or in lunches.   _____

4. I tried making homemade yogurt.   _____

5. I stopped using shortening and have switched to safflower oil.   _____

6. I put alfalfa sprouts on sandwiches and my family ate it.   _____

7. I tried making a dressing with olive oil.   _____

8. I made pizza for company and they thought it was terrific!   _____

9. I stopped buying processed cheese.   _____

10. I started buying hard cheeses without coloring.   _____

11. I started buying fresher eggs.   _____

12. I have purchased fertile eggs.   _____

13. I stopped buying plastic margarine and use butter.   _____

14. I stopped frying foods.   _____

15. I stopped buying Safflower oil from the grocery store and now buy it from a health food store.   _____

16. I stopped buying bologna and switched to cheese.   _____

17. I stopped buying peanut butter with corn syrup or sugar.   _____

18. I tried a vegetarian sandwich and liked it.   _____

19. I placed a bowl of unsalted, raw nuts out and watched my family and friends snack on them.   _____

20. My family stopped eating pork.   _____

21. I have cut down the beef consumption to once a week.   _____

22. I am now making three meatless protein balanced meals for my family a week.   _____

CHAPTER 7

MENUS

MEAT MENUS

PROTEIN BALANCED MENUS (Continued)

Bob Burgers in Pita Bread 102
Steamed Broccoli/Carrots. 56
Oven French Fries 67
Tossed Salad 79

Tacos 102
Zucchini Salad surrounded by raw vegetables. 79
Red Zinger Punch 167

Eggplant Casserole with Bulgar 102
Lettuce Plate Salad 79
Bran Muffins 30

Falafel Tacos 55
Pita Pocket Bread. 35
Raw Spinach Salad with Sunflower Seeds 80

Kidney Bean Salad. 55
Crockpot Rice Pilaf 21
Steamed Broccoli 56
Tossed Salad 79

Black Bean/Rice Soup 54
Lettuce Plate Salad 79
Cornbread. 29

Green Beans and Potatoes 52
Stuffed Eggs 111
Lettuce Plate Salad 79
Banana Bread, optional. 28

Garbanzo Beans and Rice. 54
Steamed Asparagus. 51
Fresh Vegetable Juice 163
Tossed Salad 79
Blueberry Muffins, optional. 31

Bean Soup 54
Cornbread. 29
Lettuce Plate Salad 79

Lentils over Brown Rice 62
Sesame Carrots. 57
Tossed Salad 79
Oatmeal Bread, optional. 35

PROTEIN BALANCED MENUS (Continued)   Page

CHAPTER 8

THE TRUTH ABOUT SWEETS

THE TRUTH ABOUT SWEETS

According to the dictionary, sugar is defined as "a sweet, usually crystalline, substance, $C_{12}H_{22}O_{11}$, extracted chiefly from sugar cane and sugar beets and used as a food and sweetening agent." One pound of regular white granulated sugar has no protein, no fat, no calcium, no phosphorus, no Vitamin A, B, or C. It does contain .5 milligrams of iron. It is listed as a carbohydrate, even though no distinction is made between natural carbohydrates and synthetic ones such as sugar. It can be seen that sugar is a non-nutritive empty calorie which robs the body of vitamins and minerals. It comes in assorted names such as dextrose, corn syrup, raw sugar, turbinado sugar, and malt.

HOW SWEET IT ISN'T

Because sugar lacks in the nutrition corner, obviously it doesn't contribute much to a person, except unwanted fat. Well hidden research has shown that sugar is very damaging to our bodies. Dr. John Yudkin, a noted authority on the dangers of sugar, has stated that "sugar would never be sold if it had to be proven safe." He also feels that it is not enormous amounts of sugar which are damaging, but ordinary amounts. One way it hurts our bodies is that it contributes to heart disease by causing people to eat and be overweight. Another factor in heart disease is that sugar raises the triglyceride level. And yet another point is that sugar causes blood platelets to become sticky, thus leading to blood clots and eventual heart attacks.

Important research has shown that duodenal ulcers get better when sugar is removed from the diet. The reason for this is that sugar is an irritant to the lining of the stomach and duodenum. A sugar-rich diet increases stomach acidity as much as 20 percent over a low-sugar diet.

One of the obvious causes of diabetes and hypoglycemia is an overworked pancreas. Sugar causes the pancreas to produce insulin very quickly. In the case of hypoglycemia, too much insulin is produced, thus pulling the blood sugar level too low. This continual overworking of the pancreas can lead to either disease. The old theory was to eat more sugar to regulate the pancreas; however, this tends to start the whole cycle over again bringing the blood sugar level even lower than before. Tissues become insensitive to insulin because of sugar.

Sugar causes hyperactivity because of the uncontrolled rapid absorption into blood stream. Dr. and author Lendon H. Smith has done much work to show that elimination of sugar from the diet of children can eliminate hyperactivity. Many parents will resort to dangerous drugs to control their super active children, when all they needed to do was remove the sugar bowl, and start reading labels.

It has been proven that sugar enlarges the kidneys and liver, causes an increase in uric acid in the blood, and interferes with the body's ability to break down protein. It has been said that cancer is fed by sugar.

Dental studies have proven that sugar robs the teeth of calcium, thus producing cavities. No amount of brushing in the world will bring back calcium that is drained from teeth.

With the list of diseases attributed to sugar growing day by day, it seems that sugar is not very "sweet," or kind to our bodies.

ADDICTION OF SUGAR

The more you get—the more you want! That's just the way sugar is. Many years ago when sugar was first introduced to man, only the rich could afford such luxuries. By 1840, the "sugar pushers" as William Duffy calls them in his book, *Sugar Blues;* were already passing out free samples. From there on, it was downhill all the way. These wealthy men who controlled the sugar industry determined to get everyone "hooked" on their white stuff. In fact, the sugar industries have the largest advertising in the world. Some people say that sugar is more addicting than heroin. The sad part of that statement is that there are many sincere lovely people who just can't get off sugar. They are really hooked! In fact, going off sugar has produced headaches, chills, and aches.

When you get right down to the bottom line, it is very bad to allow anything to rule your body. And yet, there are thousands of Americans who have been tricked by a group of wealthy men into consuming large quantities of their ultra-refined product. The worst part about all this is that parents allow their children to eat so much sugar without any restriction whatsoever. The increase of disease in children and young people has gone up just as the consumption of sugar has skyrocketed.

To give you an idea of how Americans satisfy their "sweet tooth," the world production of sugar climbed from 8 million to 70 million tons from 1900 to 1970. Way back in 1815 the average Englishman was only consuming about 7½ pounds of sugar each year. Now the average consumption is between 120 to 128 pounds per year. Americans are eating over 2 pounds of sugar each week. You are probably thinking that you don't eat that much sugar. But people forget that sugar is included in just about everything they eat.

BE A DETECTIVE

Only one third of a person's sugar consumption is purchased as regular packaged sugar. The other two thirds is eaten through manufactured products. Just about everything you eat, has sugar in it or is sprinkled on top when you eat it. Every box of cereal, crackers, prepared helper, fruit drinks, can of soup, TV dinners, pot pies, soft drink, flavored gelatin, pudding, some canned vegetables, catsup, hot dogs, bacon, bread, ice cream, frozen desserts, pastries, whipped toppings, dressings, mayonnaise, pickles, cream substitutes, snacks, bouillon, peanut butter, jelly, cookies, batter on frozen seafood, baby food, gravies, sauces, prepared dinners, dried soups, canned fruit, flavored yogurt, toothpaste, and even table salt, have sugar in them. The strange part about all this is that some foods are required by the FDA to have sugar in them. Catsup cannot be called catsup if it does not contain sugar. All this gives Americans a whooping two thirds of their sugar consumption and brings that sugar total over 2 pounds a week per person. How disastrous to our bodies!

Even cigarettes are cured with sugar and some people feel that the sugar in cigarettes is more damaging than the tobacco. Studies have proven that cigarettes are not only damaging for the person who smokes, but everyone around. People on a cancer control program should eliminate smoking entirely and keep it out of their home. The family who continues to smoke around a cancer patient is just plain selfish!

One of the reasons for switching to sea salt is to get rid of the sugar that is in regular table salt. Sugar is used as a cheap filler in so many products and salt is one of these. Another reason is that all minerals are taken out of regular salt, except for sodium. In fact, salt is no longer mined, but made chemically. Sea salt has all the minerals in tact, and has a good potassium/sodium balance. Sea salt is the only *natural* salt available today. Excessive salt is added to so many products, it is one of the causes of high blood pressure. Salt is mentioned many times in the Bible as a seasoning and staple ingredient of Bible days. References are Matthew 5:13, Mark 9:50, Luke 14:34 and Colossians 4:6 are just to name a few.

Studies have shown that some teenagers are getting up to 400 pounds of sugar per year. There are many teenagers who receive 50% of their daily calorie intake from sugar. In 1976, the average person consumed 20 pounds of candy, 135 sticks of gum, and 450 cans of soda pop. This explains why so much weight is lost when people stop eating sugar and start eating right.

Two of the worst sources of sugar are soda pop and boxed cereals. Even when parents are confronted with the fact that the cereal they are feeding their precious children has more sugar in it than a candy bar, they still allow the children to eat the stuff. With such a small amount of nutrients found in the sugar and injected vitamins, about the only real nutrition comes from the added milk. Sugar is listed first on many of the boxes because there is more sugar in it than cereal.

Dr. Yudkin sums up the whole subject by saying, "Sugar is pure, white, and deadly."

Once sugar is withdrawn from the diet, all foods start to taste better. Taste buds then are not geared to extreme sweetness. Soon, the craving for sugar starts to dwindle and a person feels a new freedom. In fact, when sugar has been out of the diet for awhile, a person will find that he can go for long periods without any sweet at all. It is almost as if your body relaxes and gives a big "sigh." After all, the false high is gone, the overworked pancreas can rest, and life's trials can be faced with settled nerves!

HONEY—GOD'S NATURAL SWEET

Honey is the world's oldest natural sweetener. The Bible refers to the many qualities of honey and compares it to the Word of God in Psalm 119:103, "How sweet are thy words unto my taste; yea, sweeter than honey to my mouth!" In fact, honey must have been very good for children, because in Isaiah 7:15, we read that the baby Jesus will eat butter and honey that he may know to refuse the evil, and choose the good. And then in Luke 24:42 we find the Lord Jesus eating honey again. John the Baptist is recorded living off locusts and wild honey in Matthew 3:4. David mentions honey in Psalm 19:10 and Proverbs 25:27 warns against eating much honey. It is given as a gift in Genesis 43:11, described in the taste of manna in Exodus 16:31, used to describe the Promised Land of Canaan in Exodus 3:8,17. There is a warning in Leviticus 2:11 not to use honey in a burned offering, and David is recorded as eating honey in II Samuel 17:29. Samson sees a swarm of bees and honey in the carcass of the lion in Judges 14:8. It was also used as an item of merchandise. There are sixty references to honey and honeycomb in the Bible. It was valuable and used in place of gold to pay taxes.

BEES DO ALL THE WORK

When one thinks of the work involved, honey is a remarkable natural food. In order for bees to collect one pound of honey, they must tap over 2,000,000 flowers. In this way they help pollinate. The bees keep the hives cool in the summer and warm in the winter. God even gave each little bee a radar set. Some bees travel long distances, yet always find their way back to the hive. One bee can tell the other bees where he found nectar by doing a funny little dance. From this dance, the other bees know exactly where to go. Bees live off the honey they produce.

Honey is collected from the hives by beekeepers in long flat honeycombs or frames. These wax honeycombs can be purchased already made up, so that the bees have no work in making their own honeycomb. Centrifugal force is used to spin out the honey from the comb. Some beekeepers strain their honey, although it is not necessary. Pasteurizing honey is a waste of time, because germs cannot survive in honey, but yeast cells can. It is best to buy honey that is pure, raw, unheated, unprocessed and unfiltered, because heat takes away flavor and food value.

NUTRITIONAL BREAKDOWN

Honey has nutritional value, but not in an abundant amount. It contains Vitamin C, B Complex (thiamine, pyridoxine, riboflavin), and pantothenic acid. Minerals in honey are calcium, iron, copper, with traces of sodium, potassium, magnesium, manganese, phosphorus, silica, chlorine and sulphur. It also has the enzymes diatase, inulase, catalase and invertase. The approximate breakdown of honey is as follows:

40%	levulose
34.0%	dextrose
1.9%	sucrose
17.7%	water
1.9%	dextrins and gums
0.18%	ash

Because honey is almost completely predigested when it goes into the body, it is absorbed into the blood stream and assimilated by the tissues. This means that the body can use the energy generated by honey immediately. For this reason, athletes appreciate the use of honey.

There are two different views as to the use of honey. Some authorities feel that honey is just as bad as sugar and should not be used. Even some nutritional cancer experts feel that honey is not good for the cancer patient. Other authorities such as Carlton Fredericks, Ph. D., and Dr. John Yudkin, say that honey performs as sugar in the body and is harmful. They are definitely against hypoglycemic or diabetic patients taking any honey at all. However, you can find other noted authorities such as Dr. Alan Nittler and Dr. Paavo Airola, who feel that moderate amounts of honey can be tolerated by these people with their particular health problems. I personally feel that honey reacts differently in the body than sugar. My reason for saying this is that moderate amounts of honey seem to have no effect on my body and I am able to perform much more work now than I did when I ate sugar. As every person is different, each one will have to make his own decision on honey. Since honey is a natural unrefined food, and has been around for thousands of years, I feel that moderate amounts would not be harmful.

Honey can be purchased in liquid form, or with the honey comb, or cut comb honey packaged in small cubes, or whipped honey, or solid honey which has been crystallized.

The flavors of honey range from the dark strong flavor of buckwheat to the mild light flavor of clover and alfalfa. Wildflower is a good tasting honey as well as orange blossom. Cancer patients should try to eat Tupelo honey because the flowers are only found deep in the everglades away from pollution.

There are several medicinal uses of honey. Honey mixed with lemon juice has long been a remedy for coughs. Honey has been used in baby formulas for years and it is known as a natural laxative. Bee pollen is being used by atheletes for quick energy and honey is used to rid the body of allergies.

SUBSTITUTION FOR SUGAR

Generally speaking, you may substitute ¾ cup of honey for one cup of sugar, then reduce any liquid in the recipe by ¼ cup. However, many times, you will find that the honey can be reduced even more, but this will take experimentation on your part. Use ¼ to ½ teaspoon baking soda in the recipe to neutralize the natural acidity of honey. If you measure your oil first, the honey will not stick to the cup or spoon.

Honey should be stored at room temperature, not in the refrigerator. The container should be kept in a dry cool place. Changes in temperature will cause the honey to crystallize, but this does not affect its purity or taste. To return honey to a liquid state, just place the jar in a bowl of warm water until all the crystals are melted. Honey does not freeze and excessive heat destroys the flavor and food value. Because honey is hygroscopic, that is the ability to absorb moisture from surroundings and retain it, baked goods keep much longer than those made with sugar. In fact, they have a better flavor if kept until the day after baking, before serving.

OTHER SWEETS

Molasses is an iron-rich product left from the sugar plant juice after it has been heated and sugar crystals formed. It is then removed. Blackstrap molasses has had all the sugar crystals removed. There are other sugar cane molasses such as Louisiana, Barbados, Puerto Rico, and West Indies. They vary in flavor and color. Molasses contain thiamine, riboflavin and niacin with pantothenic acid. It is high on the list of minerals with one tablespoon containing 137 mg. of calcium, 3.2 mg. of iron, 50 mg. of magnesium, 585 mg. of potassium and some chromium. It is best to use only unsulphured molasses because it's a purer product. My personal feelings about molasses are that even though it seems to be quite healthy, we are far better eating an uncooked product.

Maple syrup is similar to molasses in that it has been heated to produce the syrup. Sap is collected from maple or birch trees, and boiled down to a syrup. Here again, I feel it is better to eat a product that is uncooked.

Sorghum is another way to sweeten food. It is a member of the grass family and has been used since ancient times in China and Egypt. The syrup is made from the sweet juicy center of the stem. It is also called Broom Corn because one variety of sorghum is used in broom making. Like molasses and maple syrup, sorghum is cooked to make the syrup.

KICKING THE SUGAR HABIT

Yes

1. I have made a list of all the foods I add sugar to when I eat or drink.   _____

2. For one week, I have checked every can, package, or box to see what has sugar in it that I am now using.   _____

3. I purchased some raw honey.   _____

4. I now add a small amount of honey to my first list of foods, instead of sugar.   _____

5. I am now a detective and read every label of everything I purchase at the grocery or health food store.   _____

6. I do not buy anything with sugar in it.   _____

7. I have finally convinced my family to stop eating sugar.   _____

8. My family has started to use honey in place of sugar.   _____

9. I now make any and all desserts with honey instead of sugar.   _____

10. I have made a dessert for company that did not contain sugar.   _____

11. When I finish marking all 10 questions, "yes," I can pat myself on the back because our family has just won a tremendous victory. I now promise to stick with it.   _____

CHAPTER 9

DESSERTS

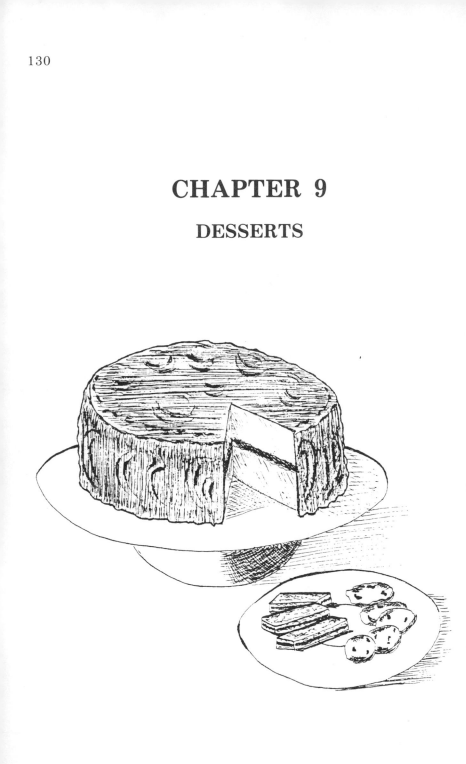

DESSERTS

How we love desserts! It seems that almost after every dinner meal we must order dessert. Even when we are stuffed, Americans must treat their "sweet tooth" to a picnic. For some people, a dessert a day makes their day. Since grown-ups feel that they need a dessert every day, now our children have adopted this policy. What Mother would pack a lunch without putting a dessert in it. Everyone has his favorite weakness. Some people have a "hang-up" on ice cream. Not a day goes by that they don't have ice cream in some form or another. Others have the chocolate chip cookie hang-up. Others are stuck on hot fudge sundaes. (That was mine.) And still others have a perpetual brownie hunger. Then there are the candy suckers, reminiscent of the pacifier days. But probably the worst of the group would be the "chocoholics."

THE GREAT AMERICAN CHOCOLATE ADDICTION

What is it that drives the average, every day, hard working, American citizen to the point that he must have chocolate or die! It is hard to understand why some people crave chocolate. Perhaps it is the caffeine that they desire or maybe it is the sugar. Some chocolate bars have as little as 10% chocolate in them. No wonder they need several to satisfy their longing—90% is filler. Last year, Americans ate 16.6 pounds of candy per person. That's a lot of candy. And that's a lot of artificial flavoring and coloring, too. Many of the beautiful, rich chocolate cake mixes contain Red Dye #2. Also the dye is in food with a brilliant red color. The FDA banned Red Dye #2 because they found that dogs were getting cancer. The dye had been used to brighten the dog food. Immediately dog food packagers stopped using the carcinogenic dye. However, "people food" manufacturers complained that the dye was in many products and they had ten years' supply of food on the shelf with Red Dye %2 in them. And so, the FDA has conveniently allowed you, the consumer, to eat ten more years of a known carcinogen.

To protect your family, you must begin to read the labels on all packaged and convenience food. When you read mono-diglycerides, sorbitan, monostearate, polysorbate 60, you can be assured that it isn't fit for a body to consume. You can imagine what happens to your tissues when you accumulate years of polysorbate 60. Many of these chemicals have a toxic level which would be dangerous to children. Instead of buying a "cardboard cake" (one that is already made up) or a "fluffy puffy cake" (one you make from a box), why not try making your own using natural ingredients. For all the chocolate lovers, here is the alternative.

CAROB

If you have never heard of Carob, I have a surprise for you. Without realizing it, you have used a word from Carob for years. The word is "carat," used to measure the weight of gem stones. This word is derived from the Arabic word, "qirat," which comes from the Greek word "keration" meaning carob bean or a small weight.

Carob appears in many ancient writings and has been used for thousands of years. The Bible does not mention the word "carob," but the prodigal son "would fain have filled his belly with the husks that the swine did eat." (Luke 15:16(These husks were actually carob pods. They are six to ten inches long. Carob is also Saint John's Bread from a tradition that John the Baptist ate this fruit in the wilderness. Carob beans are roasted and ground into a fine powder similar to cocoa. The flavor is delicious and so much like chocolate, one can hardly tell the difference. Carob has trace minerals—calcium and phosphorus, and does not interfere with calcium absorption as chocolate does. Carob does not contain caffeine. It is also very good for diarrhea.

Here is a recipe for brownies that is very good and tastes like fudge brownies. In fact, you don't have to be afraid of people not liking your brownies, they will love them!

CAROB BROWNIES

2 eggs	½ teaspoon sea salt
⅔ cup honey	1 teaspoon baking soda
½ cup melted butter	¾ cup water
1 teaspoon vanilla	⅓ cup carob, sifted
1 banana	1 cup whole wheat flour
	1 cup broken walnut pieces

Beat eggs slightly, add honey, cooled butter, vanilla and banana. Mix well. Then add the dry ingredients alternately with water. Add broken walnut pieces last. Butter and flour a 13"x9" glass baking dish and bake *exactly* 23 minutes. Do not overbake. The oven should be set at 350 degrees.

CAROB BROWNIE ICING NO. 1

⅓ cup honey	¼ cup sifted carob powder
4 tablespoons melted butter	4 tablespoons water
1 cup non-instant dry powdered milk	1 teaspoon vanilla

Mix all the ingredients together. Use the milk as a dry powder. Beat until smooth. If more water is needed, add 1 more tablespoon.

CAROB BROWNIE ICING NO. 2

4 tablespoons melted butter   ⅓ cup honey
2 teaspoons vanilla   ¼ cup sifted carob

Mix all the ingredients and beat until smooth. Can be placed on hot brownies. Also can be used as a carob syrup.

CAROB CAKE

Just double the brownie recipe and allow the cake to bake for approximately 40 minutes or until it springs back when touched. Then use either icing.

The best dessert is fruit. However, most people feel they have to offer a baked dessert to company. People on a cancer control program should use caution and have a baked dessert only on special occasions. Once a person gets away from sugar, his desire for sweets will leave. Try to get your family off desserts, by giving them fruit instead. You may also freeze one half of the dessert. This way only one half of the dessert is eaten at one time. In this way, your family will cut down on the sweets, and cut down on their individual portions. Soon you won't need many desserts at all.

There are many delicious cake recipes using fruit and vegetables as the main ingredient to give it texture or taste. Carrot Cake has been a favorite of many for years. The interesting point about carrot cake is that you don't really taste the carrots. Here is a healthy version of an old favorite.

CARROT CAKE

2 eggs   1 teaspoon baking soda
½ cup safflower oil   ¼ teaspoon sea salt
1 cup honey   1½ teaspoons cinnamon
⅓ cup yogurt   1¾ cups whole wheat flour
1 cup grated raw carrots   1 cup walnuts

Beat together the first five ingredients, gradually adding the flour, soda, salt and cinnamon. Then mix in the walnut pieces. Butter and flour a 13"x9" glass baking dish. Bake at 350 degrees for approximately 30 minutes or until cake springs back to the touch. Ice, if desired.

CREAM CHEESE ICING

8 ounces cream   ¼ cup honey
  cheese or   1 teaspoon vanilla
  goat's cream cheese

Blend together all the ingredients until smooth.

VARIATION:Add ¼ cup sifted carob to icing.

The following cake is easy to make and can be whipped up in 20 minutes with a little help from a husband. Most of the time we eat it plain without icing.

APPLE CAKE

1 cup butter
1 cup honey
3 eggs
2 teaspoons vanilla
½ teaspoon sea salt

1 teaspoon cinnamon
2 teaspoons baking soda
2 cups whole wheat flour
3 cups diced apples, peeled
  or unpeeled
2 cups walnuts, chopped

Mix together the butter, honey and eggs. Add vanilla, salt, cinnamon, and soda. Beat until smooth. Gradually add the flour. Apples can be peeled or unpeeled. Fold in the apples and walnut pieces and place in a buttered and floured 13"x9" glass baking dish. Bake at 350 degrees for 25 to 30 minutes. If icing is desired, use SPICE ICING.

SPICE ICING

⅓ cup honey
4 tablespoons melted butter
1 cup non-instant dry
  powdered milk

1½ teaspoons cinnamon
1 teaspoon allspice
1 teaspoon carob powder
4 tablespoons water
1 teaspoon vanilla

Mix all the ingredients together. Use the milk as a dry powder. Beat until smooth.

BANANA CAKE

2 eggs
½ cup butter
½ cup honey
4 medium bananas or
  1½ cups
½ teaspoon sea salt

½ teaspoon cinnamon
¼ teaspoon nutmeg
1 teaspoon baking soda
1½ cups whole wheat flour
1 cup rolled oats
1 cup chopped nuts

Beat together eggs, butter, honey and mashed bananas. Add salt, cinnamon, nutmeg and soda. Gradually add whole wheat flour. Fold in oats and nuts. Bake in 13"x9" buttered and floured baking dish at 350 degrees for 25 to 30 minutes. If icing is desired, choose one.

The next recipe is very good around the holidays. In fact, people who do not like fruit cake and have never tried natural food, will just love this. It makes an excellent gift.

HOLIDAY FRUITCAKE

2 eggs
½ cup honey
⅓ cup soft butter
2 tablespoons apple juice
½ teaspoon baking soda
½ teaspoon sea salt
1/8 teaspoon allspice
1/8 teaspoon nutmeg

½ cup whole wheat flour
2 cups walnuts, chopped
1 cup dried pineapple
½ cup dried apples
½ cup dried pears
½ cup raisins
¼ cup dried apricots

Blend eggs, honey, butter and juice. Add spices, salt and flour. Now work in all dried unsulphured fruit and walnuts. Prepare a loaf or bread pan for baking. Cut 2 lengths of waxed paper to fit down in the pan. Butter the top one. (The one underneath is just to give support when you take the fruitcake out of the pan.) Place both sheets of waxed paper into the pan with the buttered side on top. Pour batter into waxed paper, filling pan. Sides of waxed paper will come out of pan and fold over entire fruitcake. Now place the half filled bread pan into a brown paper bag and tie shut. Place a shallow pan half filled with water into a pre-heated oven of 300 degrees. Put the fruitcake that is in the bag into the pan of water and allow it to bake for one hour. After one hour, take out the pan of water and allow the fruitcake to bake an additional hour still in the brown bag. If this sounds hard, it isn't and your fruitcake will be well worth the effort. This recipe will make 1 large fruitcake or two smaller ones. Here are the directions again:

300 DEGREE OVEN
Fruitcake in waxed paper lined loaf pan
Inside a brown paper bag, tied shut
Placed in a shallow pan half filled with water

Bake 1 hour
Take out pan of water and discard
Continue baking fruitcake in paper bag for
1 Hour more

MOLASSES CAKE

1 egg	1 teaspoon cinnamon
½ cup honey	¼ teaspoon ginger
2 tablespoons butter	¼ teaspoon sea salt
⅓ cup molasses	1 teaspoon baking soda in
½ teaspoon cloves	1 cup hot water
	1½ cups whole wheat flour

Blend together the egg, honey, butter, and molasses. Add cloves, cinnamon, ginger, and salt. Gradually add flour alternately with hot water. Bake in buttered and floured 9"x9" glass baking dish for 40 minutes in an oven 375 degrees.

I do not recommend using a lot of molasses, even though it is supposed to be healthy. Cancer control persons should use caution when eating this cake and not eat very much, if any at all.

ZUCCHINI CAKE

3 large eggs	¼ teaspoon ground ginger
½ cup butter	1 teaspoon sea salt
½ cup safflower oil	2 teaspoons baking soda
1 cup honey	½ teaspoons baking powder
2 teaspoons vanilla	2½ cups whole wheat flour
3 teaspoons cinnamon	2 cups unpared, grated zucchini
	2 cups chopped walnuts

Mix together eggs, butter, oil, honey, and vanilla. Add cinnamon, ginger, salt, soda, and baking powder. Gradually add flour and grated zucchini. Fold in walnuts. Bake in a 13"x9" buttered and floured glass baking dish for 35 to 40 minutes at 350 degrees.

The following cake should only be made on special occasions and is especially good for birthday parties. It is a wonderful substitute for those gooey decorated cakes that are forced on children at parties. Children of all tastes like this cake. You can buy plastic cake decorations, birthday numbers and candles—now you are set for every birthday party that comes along.

ALMOND BIRTHDAY CAKE

½ cup butter	1 teaspoon sea salt
¾ cup honey	2 teaspoons baking soda
¾ cup buttermilk	2 cups unbleached organic flour
1½ teaspoons vanilla	¼ c. whole wheat pastry flour
2 teaspoons almond	4 egg whites, unbeaten

Cream butter and honey until well blended. Add vanilla and almond to buttermilk. Combine dry ingredients and gradually add them to honey mixture along with buttermilk. Beat well. Now add the egg whites and beat again. Butter and flour a 9"x13" glass baking dish. Bake cake for 30 minutes at 350 degrees. Frost with fluffy 7 MINUTE ICING and decorate.

7 MINUTE ICING

2 egg whites	½ cup honey
¼ teaspoon sea salt	1/8 teaspoon cream of tarter
	1 teaspoon vanilla

Place all ingredients in the top of double boiler and beat with electric mixer or egg beater for about 7 minutes or until icing stands alone in peaks.

VARIATION: Make a small cup of strong mint tea. Use 1 tablespoon in the icing and have mint icing.

One of the best ways to make a dessert even better is to add fruit to it.

APPLE CRISP

6 medium apples, sliced thin	Topping:
½ teaspoon cinnamon	1¼ cups rolled oats
½ teaspoon coriander	¾ cup whole wheat flour
raisins	¼ cup walnut pieces
¼ cup honey	¼ cup almonds
	¼ cup sesame
	¼ cup cashews

In an 8"x8"x2" glass baking dish place the sliced apples. Sprinkle cinnamon, coriander, raisins, and honey over apples. Mix the topping together and then add the following:

⅓ cup honey
¼ cup safflower oil
1 teaspoon water

Sprinkle over the apples. Now bake at 350 degrees for 35 to 40 minutes or until apples are soft.

COOKIES

No lunchbox would be complete without cookies. It seems that children really enjoy cookies more than any other dessert. A dentist once said that the sugar in store-bought cookies was worse for the teeth than any other form. Even though that statement may be hard to understand, we do know that any homemade cookie has to be better than a packaged one.

CAROB COOKIE

1 egg	1 teaspoon vanilla
⅔ cup honey	⅓ cup carob powder, sifted
½ cup butter	2¼ cups whole wheat flour
½ teaspoon sea salt	⅔ cups rolled oats
1 teaspoon baking soda	1 cup walnut pieces

Mix together the egg, honey and butter. Add sea salt, soda, and vanilla. Slowly add sifted carob powder, flour, and oats. After adding walnuts, drop by teaspoon onto buttered cookie sheet and bake at 350 degrees for approximately 10 minutes.

CARROT/PEANUT BUTTER COOKIES

⅓ cup safflower oil or butter	½ teaspoon baking soda
½ cup chunky peanut butter	1 cup carrots, grated
1 egg	¾ cup whole wheat flour
½ cup honey	½ cup instant dry milk powder
½ teaspoon sea salt	1 cup rolled oats
½ teaspoon cinnamon	½ cup raisins

Blend together the oil or butter, peanut butter, egg and honey. Mix in the salt, cinnamon, and soda. Add grated carrots and mix well. Slowly add the flour, milk powder, oats and raisins. Drop by teaspoon onto buttered cookie sheet and bake at 350 degrees for approximately 15 minutes. A cancer control person should watch his intake of peanut butter.

The next cookie is a favorite among children. Although this cookie is delicious, it must be remembered that it is baked with maple syrup, which is *not* a raw product. This cookie should only be used on very special occasions. It should not be eaten by a person on a cancer control diet.

MAPLE COOKIES

½ cup butter	¼ teaspoon sea salt
¾ cup pure maple syrup	1 teaspoon baking soda
1 teaspoon vanilla	1½ cups whole wheat flour
	2 cups rolled oats

Mix together butter, and maple syrup until smooth. Add vanilla, salt, soda and flour. Add rolled oats and drop by teasponful onto buttered cookie sheet. Bake at 325 degrees for about 15 minutes. It should make between 3 and 4 dozen cookies.

The following cookie is perhaps the most nutritious and the favorite cookie at our house.

OATMEAL COOKIES

2 eggs
¾ cup butter
1 cup honey
2 tablespoons molasses
1 teaspoon baking powder
1 teaspoon baking soda
1 teaspoon sea salt

2 teaspoons cinnamon
2 cups whole wheat flour
2 cups rolled oats—blended
1 cup rolled oats—whole
1 cup raisins
1 cup broken walnuts
1 cup sunflower seeds

Mix together the eggs, butter, honey and molasses until smooth. Add the powder, soda, salt, cinnamon and flour. In a blender or food processor, blend 2 cups rolled oats into flour. Mix the oat flour into the batter. With a spoon, stir in the cup of whole rolled oats, raisins, walnuts and sunflower seeds. Drop by teaspoon onto buttered cookie sheet and bake for 12 to 15 minutes at 350 degrees. This will make over 48 cookies.

PEANUT BUTTER COOKIES

½ cup butter
½ cup safflower oil
¾ cup honey
2 eggs

1 cup peanut butter
2 teaspoons baking soda
1 teaspoon vanilla
1 teaspoon sea salt
2½-3 cups whole wheat flour

Blend together oil, butter, honey and eggs. Mix in peanut butter. Add soda, vanilla and salt. Gradually work in flour. Form into small balls and flatten with a fork on a buttered cookie sheet. Bake between 12 and 15 minutes at 350 degrees.

REFRIGERATOR COOKIES

½ cup butter
¼ cup honey
¼ teaspoon sea salt

2 teaspoons vanilla
1 cup whole wheat flour
1 cup chopped pecans

Beat together butter and honey. Add salt, vanilla and flour. Stir in pecans. Refrigerate dough until firm enough to handle—about one hour. Roll into a log and wrap in waxed paper and refrigerate overnight. When ready to bake, use a sharp knife to slice cookies into thin rounds. Place on buttered cookie sheets and bake at 325 degrees for 15 minutes. Makes about 3 dozen.

SPICE COOKIES

1 cup butter
1 cup honey
½ teaspoon cinnamon
½ teaspoon cloves

½ teaspoon allspice
1 teaspoon baking soda
½ teaspoon sea salt
2½ cups whole wheat flour
½ cups almonds

Mix together the butter and honey. Add the spices, soda, salt and flour. Blend in the almonds. Drop by teaspoonful onto buttered cookie sheet and bake at 350 degrees for about 8 minutes.

QUICKIE BREAKFAST BAR

Step #1:

1 cup whole wheat flour
1 cup rolled oats
½ cup bran
½ teaspoon soda
½ cup honey
½ cup softened butter

Step #2:

1 cup water
2 tablespoons honey
1½ cup chopped dates
1 cup chopped nuts
½ cup sunflower seeds
1 teaspoon coriander
1/8 teaspoon cloves

Mix together the flour, otas, bran, soda, and honey in Step #1. Cut the butter into dry ingredients. Butter an 8"x8"x2" glass baking dish. Press one half of the crumbly mixture into the bottom. This layer will be thin. Bring the water to a boil with honey and dates. Boil for about 5 minutes, stirring constantly. Remove from heat, add spices, nuts. Spread mixture over the first layer. Place the rest of the crumbly mixture on top of dates to form the third layer. Bake at 350 degrees for 30 to 40 minutes. This is very rich and should be eaten in moderation. Hypoglycemia people should not eat this because of the dates. However, the following apple variation could be used, making the Quickie Breakfast Bar permissible for anyone to eat.

VARIATIONS:

Use 5 cups chopped apples for dates;
boil with ½ cup water and ¼ cup honey
Use raisins instead of dates

OATMEAL FRUIT BARS

1 egg	1/8 teaspoon cloves
½ cup butter	½ cup bran
⅔ cup honey	1 cup whole wheat flour
½ teaspoon baking soda	1½ cups rolled oats
½ teaspoon sea salt	½ cup raisins
1 teaspoon cinnamon	½ cup chopped nuts
½ teaspoon coriander	1½ cups chopped fruit

Cream egg, butter and honey. Add soda, salt, cinnamon, coriander, and cloves. Beat well. Gradually add bran, flour, and oats. Mix again. Combine fruit, raisins, and nuts with dough. Butter a cookie sheet and press dough on sheet. Bake at 350 degrees for 20 minutes until done. Cut into bars.

PIES

Since Apple Pie is so American, it seemed only natural to make a "real" apple pie with "real" flour. Once you begin working with whole wheat flour, you will find that most people enjoy the hearty taste as compared to the bland diet of white flour. You will notice that shortening is not used. Butter or safflower oil works just as good in pie crusts as shortening, which is defined in the encyclopedia as plastic materials made wholly from fats and oils.

OIL WHEAT CRUST

1 crust

1½ cups whole wheat flour	½ cup safflower oil
½ teaspoon sea salt	3 tablespoons cold water

You may sift the flour, if you like, with the salt. Also whole wheat pastry flour can be used instead of regular whole wheat, but I have used both and been successful. Blend in the oil and gradually add the ice water. If more water is needed, add to form dough. Roll out dough between two sheets of waxed paper. This will make one 9" pie crust. Carefully place crust into glass pie pan. Crimp edges. Fill with fruit and bake at proper temperature for fruit pie or bake the shell at 425 degrees for 15 to 20 minutes.

BUTTER WHEAT CRUST

2 crusts

2¼ cups whole wheat flour
¾ cup plus 1 tablespoon
    butter

1 teaspoon sea salt
⅓ cup ice water
3 tablespoons honey—optional

Sift the whole wheat flour, or use whole wheat pastry flour, with the salt. Then cut the butter into the flour until the dough is the size of peas. You may add honey, if desired. Sprinkle ice water over the dough and form into two balls. Roll out dough between two sheets of waxed paper. This will make two 9" pie crusts. Carefully place crust into glass pie pan. Fill with fruit and place other crust on top. Crimp edges. Bake at the proper temperature for whatever fruit pie you are making.

APPLE PIE

6 cups apples, thinly sliced—
    peelings on or taken off
1 whole apple, cored
½ cup honey

1 teaspoon cinnamon
    little nutmeg
1⅓ tablespoons butter
    dash lemon juice

Place whole apple, along with honey, cinnamon, nutmeg, butter and lemon juice into food processor or blender. Blend this to liquid. Arrange the 6 cups of sliced apples in unbaked pie crust and pour liquid mixture over apples. Place another pie crust or lattice work on top and cover with foil. Bake at 425 degrees for about 10 minutes and then 30 minutes at 350 degrees. Uncover the last 10 minutes.

BANANA PIE

Crust:

2 cups graham cracker crumbs
⅓ cup melted butter
2 tablespoons honey

Pie:

⅓ cup non instant milk
    powder in
⅓ cup water

2 teaspoons honey
½ teaspoon vanilla
2 very ripe bananas

Use only honey grahams from a natural food store. Check the label carefully so that they do not contain brown sugar. Make a crust with the graham cracker crumbs, butter and honey. Pat into a 9" pie shell. Mix together milk, water, honey, vanilla and bananas until smooth. Pour banana mixture into crust. Freeze and before eating, allow pie to sit at room temperature for 5 or 10 minutes.

CHEESECAKE

2 eggs plus 2 yolks	16 ounces cream cheese or
1 tablespoon vanilla	2 cups
1 tablespoon lemon juice	8 ounces plain yogurt or
	1 cup
	½ cup honey

Beat the eggs and yolks until smooth, add honey. Mix well with vanilla and lemon juice. Combine cream cheese and yogurt. Prepare CRUST as given in Banana Pie and place in 9" glass pie pan. Pour in cheesecake and bake for 40 minutes at 310 degrees. Refrigerate before eating.

PEACH PIE

4 to 5 cups sliced peaches	3 tablespoons flour
1 whole peach, pitted	¼ teaspoon cinnamon
1 teaspoon lemon juice	1 tablespoon butter
	1/8 cup honey

Place whole peach into blender or food processor along with lemon juice, flour, cinnamon, butter and honey. Arrange sliced peaches in prepared crust. Pour liquid over peaches and bake at 425 degrees for 35 minutes.

PECAN PIE

3 eggs	¼ cup butter
½ cup honey	1 tablespoon lemon juice
½ cup molasses	1 cup pecan meats

Beat eggs, honey, molasses, butter and lemon juice. Add pecans. Pour into prepared 9" pie shell. Bake at 450 degrees for 10 minutes and 350 degrees for 30 minutes.

PUMPKIN PIE

3 eggs	1 teaspoon cinnamon
1½ cups pumpkin, cooked	¼ teaspoon cloves
⅓ cup honey	¼ teaspoon nutmeg
½ teaspoon sea salt	1½ cup goat's milk or non instant milk liquid

Beat eggs. Add pumpkin and honey, mixing well. Combine spices and salt with pumpkin mixture. Slowly add milk. If you use non instant low fat milk instead of goat's milk, make the milk as you normally would and use 1½ cups liquid. Pour into prepared 9" or 10" pie shell. Bake at 425 degrees for 15 minutes and then at 325 degrees for 45 minutes.

STRAWBERRY PIE

2 cups boysenberry juice*
1½ packages unflavored
   gelatin

1 tablespoon honey
2 pints strawberries

Heat boysenberry juice until hot. Melt gelatin in juice. You may use any "red" juice instead of boysenberry. Add honey to hot juice and stir. Wash strawberries and place in pre-baked 9" or 10" pie shell. Pour cooled juice mixture over strawberries. Refrigerate until firm.

*From natural food store.

STEP-BY-STEP CHECK LIST FOR DESSERTS

Yes

1. I have tried to have fruit for dessert instead of a baked "goodie." _____

2. I have purchased carob powder _____

3. I made cookies for my children's lunches. _____

4. I made a cake and served it to my family. _____

5. I made Holiday Fruit Cakes for Christmas and gave them as gifts. _____

6. I made a pie for my family. _____

7. I served a dessert for my guests made with natural ingredients. _____

8. I took brownies someplace and people enjoyed eating them. _____

9. I have switched from a "sugary" birthday cake to a more natural one. _____

10. I am using carob instead of chocolate. _____

11. I am making my own cakes instead of buying them. _____

12. I am now using butter instead of margarine. _____

13. I am making my own cookies or buying non-sugar ones from the health food store. _____

14. I am using glass baking dishes, pyrex, or Corning Ware instead of aluminum. _____

15. I now buy pure vanilla instead of imitation. _____

CHAPTER 10

SNACKS

SNACKS

Snacks are an important part of every child's diet. The reason for this is that children are continually snacking. When they come in from school, they immediately go to the kitchen for something to nibble on. Two minutes after supper, they want to eat again. As parents, we must have nutritious snacks available for them.

One of the deadly snacks is ice cream. Very few companies are using "real fruit" as flavoring in ice creams. The flavors are just chemicals, which taste like bananas, strawberries, etc. Another area of garbage food is all the little bags of candies and goodies that children buy at convenience stores. The sad part about it is that some kids practically live off the junk from these stores. Of course soda pop and flavored water drinks are a big part of the snack line-up.

Every snack that has a chemical in it should have a warning label that it is dangerous to your health. Since Americans consume 22 pounds of chemicals per year, some people may reach their saturation point even while reading this book. There isn't too much hope for the younger generation. Our hospitals will soon be filled with people in their twenties suffering from "Junkitis."

To give you a small idea of what these flavors are, here is a partial list:

Banana is Amyl-acetate
Cherry is Aldehyde C-17
Pineapple is Ethyl-acetate
Strawberry is Benzyl-acetate
Vanilla is Piperonal
(lice killer in chicken coops)

Now, you might have a different idea the next time someone gives you a dish of ice cream. The sad part about this fake food is that people are paying money for it and thinking they are getting food!

BE PREPARED

The whole key to snacks is to BE PREPARED! Go out of your way to have wholesome snacks. Dr. Lendon H. Smith tells mothers to give their children peanut butter instead of sugar when they come home from school. He explains in his book, *Improving Your Child's Behavior Chemistry,* how the behavior of a child is directly related to what he eats. Dr. Smith says that the reason children are so hyperactive today is that they are getting too much sugar.

Another pioneer in the work of relating diet to behavior is Dr. Benjamin Feingold, who wrote the book, *Why Your Child is Hyperactive.* Children who were really "uncontrollable" are now little "angels" because of their switch in diet. Feingold kids, as they are called, are not allowed to eat artificial colors, artificial flavors, chemical additives like BHA, BHT, MSG, and salicylates which are in aspirin, wintergreen and certain vegetables and fruits such as berries, peaches and tomatoes. By eliminating artificial food, the sugar is decreased by enormous amounts and this definitely helps to eliminate hyperactivity. Their stories are miraculous and prove that diet does have something to do with behavior. It has been stated that about 15% or six million children in the U.S. are suffering from hyperactivity.

HOLIDAYS

Many people ask, "but what do we do about holidays?" It's easy, BE PREPARED. Once your child has eliminated sweets from his diet, he will begin to lose his craving for sugar. You will, of course, be feeding this child other delicious snacks and substitutes. And you will be talking and explaining to him how harmful some food is to his body. You can involve the child in making his own snacks and prasing him for choosing nutritious food over junk. Every couple of weeks, you will let him pick out a snack at a natural food store, but read the label! Make an outing one day and take the children to a health food store that serves honey ice cream or yogurt. Friday night at the mall is always topped off with a honey yogurt ice cream cone. My children aren't left out, they feel special and want to help spread the news of nutritious food.

When holidays come, I start looking for candy bars made with carob and honey, hard candies made with honey, sesame stix, sugarless mints, and gum, and a nice selection of nuts and fruits. They are just as proud of their selection of goodies as the other children.

Parties at school and church are easy, if you know in advance. We prepare for the party by allowing the child to decide what she wants to take to eat. Sometimes I narrow the selection down to about three things. Well, it's a big decision, but finally the child settles on just the right snack and then we make it. One time it may be Brownies and the next time Peanut Butter Balls, but I always make sure a happy child goes out the door with the snack that *she* wants. We always send a small bottle of fruit juice with a straw, and if the other children are eating a lot, we send popcorn and a sandwich. School parties are usually light—snack and drink. Birthday parties are snack, drink, and popcorn. Church parties sometimes involve snack, drink, and sandwich. Just ask ahead of time so that you are prepared. Children become discouraged when they are eating a small snack and the other kids have sandwiches.

Staying overnight at a friend's house is a little more involved. First of all, talk to the other mother and explain your views. Ask her what she was planning on having for supper. Many times it will be all right to eat, if your child asks for water instead of tea, no bread and no dessert. If the slumber party eating involves pizza or hot dogs, chips and pop, then it is fairly easy. That night for your own family's supper, just make homemade pizza. Have a nice big piece all wrapped up for your child to take to the slumber party. Almost all health food stores carry beef or chicken hot dogs without nitrates. Send a couple of these along. They also carry potato chips with sea salt, fried in safflower oil and honey root beer and other soda pops. Many times, my girls have carried their own hot dogs, chips and root beer to a party. They have the same thing as all the other children, but I have the assurance it is made a little better without sugar and chemicals with better ingredients. They do not feel slighted or discouraged. In fact, they explain to the other children how good natural food is for them. Many times other children will try to trade a store bought cardboard cookie for some natural goodie my girls carry in their lunches. Children are easy to convince when it comes to eating right. It's the grown ups who are stuck in their eating habits.

Sometimes, it has been necessary on all night camping trips for my girls to take all of their food. Here again, we make it extra special. Many little sugarless surprises are packed in with the food to encourage them. They feel so special by the time they leave that there is never any thought of "cheating" and getting into sugar away from home. Of course, all this extra food is bothersome for the leaders. But if they want my girls to be involved, then they have to take our natural food. Often times, leaders and teachers will be so relieved when I say that I will send my child's food. Somehow they got the idea that they would have to provide for them.

Halloween is a little harder than the other holidays. I have worked up a plan that is very exciting and my girls just love it. In fact, they can hardly wait to Halloween. Here is the outline:

SUGGESTIONS FOR HALLOWEEN
GIVE OTHER CHILDREN BETTER TREATS

Popcorn	Sugarless gum
Popcorn & honey balls	Apples
Peanuts	Pennies
	Raisin Boxes

HOW TO HANDLE YOUR OWN CHILDREN'S HALLOWEEN TREATS

1. Before Halloween make or buy some of the "good" treats your children like. This will be your "Natural Goodie Store" explained later on.

2. Allow them to go "Trick or Treating" just in your neighborhood to people you know.

3. Give each piece of candy in their bag a value. Some are worth 2^c, 5^c, and some 10^c. Spread them all out into the proper categories.

4. Now, buy the candy from the child. Every year each child has brought home about $3.60 worth of candy. Since you own the candy, do whatever you want with it. (I threw out mine.)

5. Open up your "Natural Goodie Store" and let your children buy whatever they want from you. They always have money left over and will enjoy spending the rest of their money on a new toy, etc.

If you have more children and don't feel that you can afford to pay the children for the candy, just appropriate a smaller amount for each piece of candy. This will cut down on your cost, but the children will still get some money to buy goodies from you.

The peanut butter listed on the SNACK LIST is meant to be freshly ground peanut butter from a health food store, not the "corn syrup" kind from the grocery store. I don't advocate eating a lot of peanut butter. According to most authorities, almost all peanuts are grown having an aflotoxin fungus on them. Cancer control patients should be very cautious of the amount of peanut butter eaten.

SNACK LIST

Fresh Fruit	Nuts	Seeds	Miscellaneous
Apples	Almonds	Sunflower	Popcorn
Bananas	Brazil	Sesame	Sesame Stix
Oranges	Cashews	Pumpkin	Yogurt
Grapes	Hazel	Squash	Honey Ice Cream
Peaches	Peanuts		Homemade Popsicles
Plums	Pecans		Peanut Butter Balls
Tangerines	Pistachio		Peanut Butter Sandwich
Apricots	Macadamia		Crackers/cheese
Pears	Walnuts		Honey Graham Crackers
			Homemade Cookies
			Homemade Desserts
Dried Fruit			Celery sticks
Apples			Carrot sticks
Apricots			Fruitsicles
Coconut			
Dates			
Figs			
Pears			
Pineapples			
Prunes			
Raisins			

PEANUT BUTTER BALLS

½ cup honey   1 cup non instant powdered
½ cup peanut butter   milk not made into a liquid
                                                     Unsweetened coconut

Mix together the honey, peanut butter and milk powder. Mold into small balls and roll in coconut. Store in the refrigerator.

VARIATIONS:
Add ¼ cup sunflower seeds
Add ¼ cup raisins
Add ¼ cup sesame seeds
Add ¼ cup walnuts
Add ¼ cup pecans
Add ¼ cup carob

FRUITSICLES

Pour undiluted fruit juice into ice cube tray or popsicle containers. When half frozen insert clean popsicle sticks or craft sticks. Continue freezing. Eat when entirely frozen.

Grape	Cherry	Boysenberry	Apple
Pineapple	Orange	Blackberry	Strawberry

GELATIN

1 package unflavored gelatin	½ cup fruit
2 cups fruit juice	¼ cup nuts, optional

Heat fruit juice until hot and pour over gelatin. Mix until dissolved. Add desired fruit and nuts. Refrigerate.

VARIATIONS:
Grape juice, grapes and walnuts
Apple juice, apples and walnuts
Cherry juice, and cherries or strawberries
Grape juice, bananas and walnuts

SPICE CANDY

⅔ cup honey	3 teaspoons cinnamon
½ cup butter	2 teaspoons carob powder
2 cups non-instant dry powdered milk	8 tablespoons water
2 teaspoons allspice	2 teaspoons vanilla
	½ cup pecan pieces

Mix all the ingredients together. Use the milk as a dry powder. Beat until smooth. Butter a 10"x6" glass dish and press in candy. Cut into small pieces. Refrigerate.

VARIATION:
CAROB CANDY—eliminate cinnamon, allspice and carob powder, add ¼ cup carob.

FROZEN YOGURT

1 package unflavored gelatin	⅓ cup honey
2 tablespoons boiling water	⅓ cup non-instant powdered milk
2 cups plain yogurt	1½ cups strawberries

Pour boiling water over gelatin and make sure it gets dissolved. Place yogurt, honey, powdered milk and gelatin in blender and blend. Add the strawberries and blend more.

ICE CREAM MAKER METHOD: Place into ice cream freezer and churn as you would other ice cream.

FREEZER METHOD: Put yogurt into freezer and when partially frozen, but still soft in the center, remove from freezer and beat again until smooth. Either use mixer, food processor or blender. Return to freezer and eat when frozen.

SOFT FROZEN YOGURT: Allow yogurt to sit out 20 to 30 minutes before serving to soften.

VARIATION:
Use 1 cup blueberries
Use 1½ cups peaches
Freeze yogurt in popsicle containers for Yogurt Pops

GOAT'S MILK ICE CREAM

1 egg	3 cups goat's milk
½ cup whipping cream	2 teaspoons vanilla
½ cup honey	

Beat egg. Add honey, goat's milk, and vanilla. Beat in whipping cream for a few seconds. Place in ice cream treezer. It makes 1 quart.

VARIATIONS:

CAROB—1/8 cup carob added or 2 tablespoons

STRAWBERRY—2 cups strawberries added

POWDERED MILK ICE CREAM

1 egg	2½ cups instant powdered
1 cup whipping cream	milk made into liquid
½ cup honey	2 teaspoons vanilla

Beat egg. Add honey, milk, and vanilla. Beat in whipping cream for a few seconds. Place in ice cream freezer. It makes 1 quart.

A new type of ice cream freezer has been developed. Salton makes a very nice electric freezer like this. It is simple to use and is placed inside the freezer with the cord coming out, plugged into the electrical outlet.

BIRTHDAY PARTY MENU

ALMOND BIRTHDAY CAKE with 7 MINUTE ICING
VANILLA ICE CREAM

NUT CUP

FRUIT PUNCH

ALMOND BIRTHDAY CAKE—page 136 decorated with candles, and plastic figurines, birthday numbers, toys or artificial flowers. A purchased cake ruffle can be placed around the bottom of the cake.

7 MINUTE ICING—page 137

VANILLA ICE CREAM—page 153

NUT CUP—consisting of peanuts, cashews, sunflower seeds, and sesame stix. Individual ruffled paper cups can be used.

FRUIT PUNCH—page 165

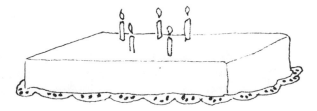

STEP-BY-STEP CHECK LIST FOR SNACKS

Yes

1. I have thrown out all candy and replaced it with
   wholesome snacks.   ____

2. Our family purchased honey yogurt or honey ice cream at a
   health food store.   ____

3. I sent my child's snacks to a party.   ____

4. I got through my first holiday without candy in
   our house.   ____

5. I tried the Halloween Plan and it worked!   ____

6. For one week my child came home from school and
   had a wholesome snack.   ____

7. I served good snacks to guests and they ate it.   ____

8. I had a birthday party and it was a success.   ____

CHAPTER 11

BEVERAGES

BEVERAGES

What is a picnic without soda pop? Or what is a party without a soft drink? People can't have fun anymore unless they drag along a bottle of pop. It is nothing for children to consume large quantities of soda at social gatherings. Vending machines seem to cough up tons of aluminum on college campuses, high schools, grade schools, hospitals, ball games, beaches, churches, gas stations, motels, and just about any where else people go. How many times have you seen a child or adult order a soft drink with his meal at a restaurant. We get so much advertising to drink the stuff that it seems "unnatural" not to drink it. After all, if you're in the Pepsi generation, then you know that things go better with Coke. These companies are the largest advertisers the world over.

Isn't it strange that the most persuasive advertising is wanting us to drink something that isn't really good for us.

CONSUMPTION OF SODA POP

Way back in 1849, when soft drinks began emerging around the country, very few people drank the stuff. In fact during the whole year, there was only 1.6 eight ounce containers consumed per person in the U.S. in one year. Then around 1900 the total consumed per person rose to 12.2 eight ounce containers. Then in 1940 the total was 100.1 eight ounce containers per person a year. In the fifties, the total grew to 158.0 per person. In 1960 the total per person was 192 and in 1974, it was 432. Now the total eight ounce containers consumed by each person per year is well over 500 cans. This means that the soft drink consumption has risen in the past ten years from 2,500 million gallons to 5,500 million gallons. That is a lot of sugar and chemicals for Americans to consume. No wonder we have so many ailments!

A survey was made at the Pennsylvania State University as to the consumption of cokes by their students. The survey revealed that some of these students were drinking up to 111 ounces of coke each day or about 14 bottles. Many students admitted that they could not live without soft drinks. One professor was shocked to learn that a girl had consumed 37 cokes in two days while studying for an English examination.

Boys Life magazine surveyed its readers and discovered that 8% of them drank 8 or more bottles of soda pop a day. Conventions, meetings, camp grounds, and social gatherings always produce a collection of aluminum cans. One Boy Scout Jamboree coughed up 200,000 cans for recycling.

Dale Alexander, a well known nutritionist, boldly exclaims that soft drinks are the number one cause of cancer. Whether this is true or not, one does not know. However, we must agree with Mr. Alexander that something in our bodies must have changed drastically when we went from drinking one and a half cans of soda pop per year to 500 cans.

How proudly the Soft Drink Association boasts that 85 percent of the hospitals they surveyed serve soft drinks routinely to their patients. Is it any wonder that we can't get well. Here are very sick people being served soft drinks that do not contain one ounce of anything nourishing. They could be served raw vegetable juices, fruit juices and herb teas. These contain vitamins and minerals to help heal the body.

ADDICTION OF SODA POP

You might laugh when you see that title "Addiction of Soda Pop." Maybe you are a person who thinks there is no such thing. Yet, in this fast moving world we are sad to report, there are alcoholics, chocoholics, and coffeeholics and sodaholics. We frown on the alcoholic because he cannot control his desire for alcohol. But is it any less a sin to be so addicted to other forms of stimulants?

Some people cannot live without soft drinks. Is it any wonder we are rearing a generation of "pop guzzlers?" Children are encouraged to drink soft drinks when they come home from school or come in from play. They claim, "I am so thirsty! Please let me have some soda." Soft drinks have taken the place of water for many children. Students are notorious for consuming large quantities of pop. When interviewed, they claim, "I just can't live without it."

Those people really addicted to soft drinks suffer withdrawal type symptoms when they stop drinking it. Some experience depression, nervousness and decrease in alertness. One person I observed had to return to her normal consumption of soda after one and a half days of headache. She just couldn't take the withdrawal.

Perhaps here it would be good to remind ourselves that in I Corinthians 3:16-17 there is good advice:

Know ye not that ye are the temple of God, and that
the Spirit of God dwelleth in you? If any man defile
the temple of God, him shall God destroy; for the
temple of God is holy, which temple ye are.

A former professor of medicine at Vanderbilt University and one time president of the AMA, John Witherspoon, M.D., is quoted in

Fact, Nov./Dec., 1964 as saying, "Young people soon form the habit of taking Coca Cola and take sometimes 8, 10, 15 or 20 drinks a day. They really look like morphine habitues, so far as their efforts to control it are concerned. I have treated probably 30 or 40 patients afflicted with the Coca Cola habit during the last 4 or 5 years. I have had 3 cases in the hospital that I tried to break of the habit . . . I regard Coke as habit forming; one glass creates a demand for another because it stimulates the user and makes him feel better; then, when its effect wears off, the reaction is one of depression, and he gets very nervous and seemingly cannot do without it."

In *The Big Drink* by E. J. Kahn, a Coke research man said, "You can drink Coke every day all day long and not get tired of it. Fifteen minutes after you've finished a Coke, you're a new customer again, and that's where we get you."

WHY BE A SLAVE

As you are reading this, perhaps you can identify and see yourself among these examples. You know you have a problem. Don't give up. And please don't be upset or angry. Usually soda pop drinkers do not get angry when confronted with the truth. (The coffee drinkers do though!) Just keep on trying to give up the soda, if that is what you want to do. I have heard of a child who was taken off soft drinks, but because the withdrawal was so bad, the doctor ordered him back to the soda pop. Can you imagine what he is like now as an adult? Don't be a slave to anything. "Kick" the habit before it "kicks you," and you "kick the bucket!"

WHY ARE SOFT DRINKS SO DEADLY?

The United States Department of Agriculture confesses that soft drinks comprise the largest single use of *refined sugar*. This means that over one-fifth of the total intake of sugar in the American diet is from soft drinks. Sugar is discussed in chapter eight.

The American Dental Association has something to say about soft drinks. "All sweetened beverages, and cola drinks more than the others, substantially decay teeth, cause dental plaque, and eat away the tooth enamel." There are many different types and amounts of sugars in all soda. Another tooth destroyer is phosphoric acid. Some experts feel that small amounts of cola at frequent intervals is just as bad as larger amounts taken at once.

Another harmful ingredient in soft drinks is the *caffeine*. It is not to exceed .02% by weight. In one small bottle of Coke, there are about 40 milligrams of caffeine. Three small bottles would equal the caffeine in one cup of coffee. One Dutch physician did a study and discovered that the caffeine in cold drinks is far more potent than that in hot or warm drinks. So, we can conclude that the caffeine in soft drinks is more deadly than in hot coffee or tea.

There are over 679 *artificial flavorings* permitted in soft drinks. These flavorings are chemicals used to create a certain taste—all of them are a fake! They may be added in a carrier consisting of ethyl alcohol, glycerin, or propylene glycol.

And if that isn't enough chemicals, there are natural and *artificial color additives* and *dyes*. These are used to get cherry soda, red and grape soda, purple, etc.

Then there are the *acidifying agents*. These might be acetic acid, adipic acid, citrus acid, fumaric acid, lactic acid, malic acid, phosphoric acid or tartaric acid.

What about the *buffering agents?* These might be acetate bicarbonate, chloride citrate, lactate orthophosphate or sulfate salts of calcium, magnesium, potassium or sodium.

Now we have *emulsifying, stabilizing* or viscosity producing *agents*. These may be brominated vegetable oil, carob bean gum, glycerol ester of wood rosin, guar gum, gum acacia, gum tragacanth, hydroxylated lecithin, lecithin, methylcellulose, mono—and di-glycerides of fat forming fatty acids, pectin, polyglycerol esters of fatty acids, propylene glycol alginate, sodium alginate, sodium carboxymethylcellulose, and sodium metaphosphate.

Then there are the *foaming agents*. These may be ammoniated glycyrrhizan, gum ghatti, licorice or glycyrrhiza, yucca, or quillaia.

Quinine is in soda not to exceed 83 parts per million.

And we cannot forget the *preservatives*. They are ascorbic acid, benzoic acid, BHA, BHT, calcium disodium, EDTA, erythorbic acid, glucose-oxidase-catalase enzyme, methylparaben or propylparaben, proply gallate, potassium or sodium benzoate, potassium or sodium bisulfite, potassium or sodium metabisulfite, potassium or sodium sorbate, sorbic acid, sulfer dioxide or tocopherols. And in canned soda we have stannous chloride not to exceed 11 parts per million.

Lastly we have the *defoaming agent* which is dimethylpolysiloxane in an amount not to exceed 14 parts per million.

All of the above ingredients were listed in the *National Register* published by the FDA on August 11, 1970. Now, perhaps you can see why soft drinks are so deadly. Every time your child starts to drink a soda pop, you are allowing him to poison his body.

COFFEE, TEA OR MILK?

Do we really need that much coffee, tea, and milk? It seems that whatever Americans eat, they tend to overdo. Probably the reason our country has such a high rate of cancer is because we "over eat" everything we like. Moderation seems to be the key in many of our health related activities.

Americans are drinking less coffee. According to the International Coffee Organization, in 1950, coffee drinkers comprised 77.4 percent of the population. But by 1977, that figure had dropped to 57.9 percent. Milk consumption is declining even more drastically. Possibly, these people are turning to soda pop.

Dr. Atkins feels that people who drink the most coffee, between 8-10 cups a day are the ones who usually need to get off the coffee. He says that these people many times are the ones with hypoglycemia or low blood sugar.

Usually "coffeholics" won't admit that they are hooked on coffee. If they only realized the effect of the continual caffeine supply to their body, they would want to stop. Coffee robs the body of B vitamins and causes breathlessness. When a person says, "I am drinking coffee for my nerves," he must mean that he is drinking coffee to make his nerves worse; since coffee destroys the nerve building vitamins. Coffee drinking has been linked to bladder cancer. Almost all bladder cancer patients said they drank a lot of coffee. Another strike against coffee is that it contains factors which act as catalysts for the formation of nitrosamines from nitrites. Nitrites or nitrates are preservatives and coloring agents used in hot dogs, ham and bologna. The conclusion we can see is not to combine coffee and nitrites. Decaffeinated coffee isn't much better than regular in that Trichloroethylene (TCE) is employed to flush the coffee bean. TCE is also used in dry cleaning and degreasing machine parts.

Incidentally, those "international style" coffees are 53% sugar, 27% fat and contain at least 10 artificial chemicals. What's even worse is that it sells for $18.00 a pound.

ALTERNATIVE TO COFFEE

There are several "coffee-like" drinks, which are very good. When our ancestors headed out across America on the Oregon Trail, they could not get coffee. They substituted roasted barley and chicory. These are the main ingredients in two hot drinks called "Pero" and "Caffix." A perked-type drink like coffee is called "Heritage." You can find these or perhaps one similar, at your natural food store.

TEA

So many people say that tea is worse than coffee. Perhaps the culprit is "Theobromine" which does about the same thing that caffeine does to the body. Weight for weight, tea leaves have more than twice as much caffeine as coffee beans, but a cup of coffee generally has more of the alkaloid than a cup of tea. Tea also contains Tannic acid. And yet, many people feel that drinking tea all day long isn't quite as bad as drinking coffee. But what about the thousands of children across America who are given large glasses of ice tea? Can this be healthy for those children?

MILK

And now we come to milk. There are some parts of America where doctors ask their patients not to drink milk. The reason for this turn from milk is *radiation* fallout. Doctors have agreed for some time that we do not need as much milk as we have been led to believe. Also, the new school teaches that milk is unnecessary past a certain age, because children have an enzyme called "rennin" which aids digestion. Adults do not have this enzyme.

Lately there have been reports about poisonous DDT spray found in milk. Another strike against milk has been chemicals used to preserve it. Of course, if a person could get raw milk, then there wouldn't be a problem with preservatives. However, raw milk is illegal, unless it is certified. Some parts of the country have "Kosher style" milk. Supposedly this milk is just brought to the pasteurization point. It is not injected with vitamins, nor preservatives. Skim milk has so much taken out of the original milk, that there is little benefit from drinking it. Buttermilk could be a healthy drink considering the acidophilus bacteria in it and B vitamins. However, caution must be given. Some buttermilk is not as good as others because it is a commercially cultured product. Many people have turned to the non instant lowfat powdered milk from a natural food store. The non instant varieties of this milk are sun dried or dried by a low heat method.

NON-INSTANT LOWFAT POWDERED MILK

1 quart water   1⅓ cups milk powder

Blend until smooth. Use in place of milk.

What can a person do about drinking milk? If you want to continue to drink milk, why not try goat's milk? Boy that's a shock! One redeeming quality about goat's milk is that it is much easier to digest than cow's milk. It can be used in any recipe calling for milk. Goat's milk is much like cow's milk in nutritive value. When the milk is cooled quickly, its flavor improves. There are small fat globules and soft curds in goat's milk, which make it easy to digest. Some breeds have milk which is 4.0 to 6.0 percent butterfat.

If you are on a cancer prevention diet, then try to cut your intake of milk way down and consider some of the alternatives already discussed. If you are on a cancer control diet, then you will want to stay clear of milk, with the exception of goat's milk. You will notice very few recipes calling for milk throughout this book.

WHAT CAN WE DRINK?

Fruit juices are the best substitute for soda pop, if something sweet is desired. Many people do not drink enough plain 'ole water and especially some children. But when the children do crave soft drinks, hand them a glass of unsweetened grape juice. When a child is going to a party, give him a small bottle or can of unsweetened pineapple juice, apple juice or grape juice to carry along. Instead of serving soda pop at the next party, try apple cider.

Studies have shown that during a meal, a person should not drink any liquid. The food should be chewed completely working the gums and allowing the saliva to begin breaking down the food. "Washing" down the food with a drink is not good for the body.

Check all labels on fruit juices. Make sure the labels read "unsweetened" and "no preservatives added." Also choose juices that do not have vitamins added. Instead of reaching for a "kool-aid" type drink that is mostly sugar with artificial flavoring, look next to it and get a natural juice. Then check your local natural foods store for some extra special juices. You may use these to make gelatin and fruitsicles, which are discussed in SNACKS.

Vegetable juices are an excellent source of vitamins and minerals. Many people have come back from near death because they drank fresh raw vegetable juices. If you don't have a juicer, you should look into buying one. There are many wonderful combinations for raw juices. Carrots, celery, and parsley make a good drink. People on a cancer control diet should have lots of raw juices. Since they have eliminated coffee, tea and milk, raw juices could be used every day without any problem.

Your grocery store will have many juices which you can buy. Try to choose bottled juices over cans. You should be able to find the following:

> Unsweetened grape juice
> Unsweetened apple juice
> Unsweetened apple cider
> Unsweetened pineapple juice
> Unsweetened orange juice
> Unsweetened grapefruit juice
> Unsweetened prune juice
> Unsweetened tomato juice

It is almost impossible to find pineapple juice in a bottle, except at the health food store. Those persons on a cancer control diet should only drink juices fresh and from a glass bottle. They also should restrict their intake of citrus juice to not more than one small glass a day. Orange juice should be freshly squeezed.

Your local health food store should have quite a large selection of delicious bottled juices. Here are a few that you could choose from:

> Apple
> Apricot
> Banana/Pineapple
> Blackberry
> Boysenberry
> Cherry
> Cranberry
> Grape
> Peach
> Pear
> Pineapple
> Raspberry
> Strawberry

Many of these concentrated drinks will have apple juice in them. However, they can be diluted to suit your taste. They also come in small bottles to send with your children for a special party or picnic. In fact, you can even buy honey sweetened root beer, when your child feels that he has to have soda pop.

If you get tired of drinking plain water, try adding a little lemon juice to it. It is a very good thirst quencher and you do not need any sweetener if you go lightly on the lemon juice.

FRUIT PUNCH

1 qt. boysenberry or
  cherry juice
4 cups apple cider

½ qt. ice water
½ cup lemon juice

An ice ring can be made by slicing lemons and limes and placing them in
a ring mold partially filled with water to freeze. When filling the ring to
the top, add strawberries.

Punch is easy to make because you can use just about any fruit juice
you have. Begin with some juice that is very sweet and strong flavored
like boysenberry, cherry, or grape juice. Then add something with a little zip to it like lemon juice or orange juice. Add a little water and keep
tasting. If you want a lot of bubbles in it, buy a lemon flavored honey
sweetened soda pop from the health food store and that will do the
same thing as ginger ale.

HOT APPLE CIDER

1 gallon unsweetened
  apple cider
1 teaspoon whole cloves

4 cinnamon sticks
1 teaspoon whole allspice

Heat the cider for about 20 minutes. Then strain or dip out the spices.
Slice one orange studded with cloves and float in apple cider.

HOT FRUIT PUNCH

2 qts. apple cider
2 cups orange juice
2 cups pineapple juice

1 teaspoon whole allspice
1 teaspoon whole cloves
3 cinnamon sticks

Heat every ingredient for about 20 minutes. Strain the spices and serve
hot.

A refreshing drink either hot or cold is Cinnamon Tea. It is a
natural "picker-upper." You can either buy the cinnamon sticks from
the grocery store or from the health store, where they are cheaper. For
those on a "cancer control" diet, don't drink very much of this.

CINNAMON TEA

5 cinnamon sticks

Pot of water

Boil water and drop in sticks. Turn to medium or low and simmer for
about 20 minutes. Tea should be dark. Store in refrigerator. Add water if
you don't want it so strong. Sometimes the sticks can be reused to get
more mileage out of them.

SHAKES AND DRINKS

Now that you are getting used to fruit juices, you can make fruit shakes with the help of a blender. There are very good books published that give many ideas for shakes. Here are a few of the combinations we like best.

BANANA ORANGE JUICE DRINK

1 banana   ¾ cup apple juice
1 cup orange juice

Blend all three ingredients until mixed. If you are on a cancer control diet, keep the orange juice to a minimum or substitute another juice.

BANANA STRAWBERRY SHAKE

1 banana   10 frozen strawberries
5 ice cubes   1 cup apple juice
2 tablespoons yogurt   1 tablespoon protein
                                       powder (optional)

Blend banana, apple juice, plain yogurt and protein powder. When mixed, add ice cubes and strawberries. If you want a thinner shake, add water.

If you decide to kick the milk habit and want a substitute, here is a simple, but very nourishing milk. It is excellent for a cancer control diet, as sesame seeds are a good source of nitrilosides.

SESAME SEED MILK

1 pint water   ½ cup sesame seeds

Blend ¼ cup seeds until powder, add ¼ cup more with a little water. Then add the rest of the water and refrigerate. Use like milk.

HOMEMADE BUTTERMILK

Mix 1⅓ cups instant non-fat powdered milk from the Health food store with 1 quart of water. Do not chill. Then stir in ½ cup buttermilk and a pinch of salt. Cover and let stand at room temperature until clabbered over night. Stir until smooth and keep refrigerated. Remember to save ½ cup buttermilk for your next batch.

HOT CAROB FOR 2

Place 2 cups goat's milk in sauce pan on low heat. Add 2 to 3 teaspoons carob, and stir. Add dash of honey, if desired. When warm, remove from heat and serve.

HOW ABOUT A CUP OF HERB TEA?

If you are used to drinking a gallon of ice tea every day like I used to, don't expect to find an herb tea to replace your tea habit. There just isn't one. But don't lose hope, your taste buds will change and you will find that you can get along without all that tea. When you check into your local health food store and find at least 37 different varieties of herb teas, you'll probably say, "Oh no! Which one should I buy?" Don't buy any until you read the labels and talk to other people to find out what is good. Be sure to try them hot and cold. Here is our favorite.

RED ZINGER HERB TEA

¼ cup Red Zinger Tea
4 cups apple juice or
   apple cider
¼ cup fresh lemon juice

Bring a pot of water to a boil and add herb tea. Turn off and allow the tea to steep for about 20 minutes. In gallon pitcher, place ice, lemon juice, apple juice and strained Red Zinger Tea. Fill with water. Since the apple juice sweetens this drink, you don't need anything else but more apple juice if you want it sweeter. It tastes similar to pink lemonade.

The contents of Red Zinger Tea are rosehips, hibiscus flowers, lemon grass, peppermint, orange peel, wild cherry bark, and wintergreen. This drink would be a good source of Vitamin C.

For hot tea, we usually drink gossip tea, peppermint tea, lemon mist tea, pelican punch, or raspberry leaves. The raspberry leaves are supposed to be very good whenever you have a cold or flu. And the peppermint tea will calm an upset stomach. Genseng Tea is from the Orient and helps many ailments. Chamomile tea will induce sleep. Chaparral Tea should be used by cancer patients.

COLD HERB TEAS

Use at least 3 to 4 tea bags or ¼ cup loose tea for ½ gallon of water. Either sweeten with honey in the hot tea or try to sweeten with fruit juice. Experiment until you find the taste you like.

STEP-BY-STEP CHECK LIST FOR BEVERAGES

Yes

1. I have stopped buying "kool aid" type drinks for the children and am buying fruit juices. _____

2. I have sent juice to a party for my children. _____

3. I have served fruit juice instead of soda pop for company. _____

4. I have cut down my consumption of soft drinks to one half of what it used to be. _____

5. I have cut down my soft drinks to only one per week. _____

6. I do not have to drink soft drinks and can now choose juice or water without any problem. _____

7. I have cut my coffee consumption to one cup per day. _____

8. I have tried going without coffee. _____

9. I have tried a coffee substitute. _____

10. I have cut down my tea consumption to one glass a day. _____

11. I have tried to drink water when eating out instead of drinking tea. _____

12. I have tried cold herb tea. _____

13. I have tried hot herb tea. _____

14. I have cut down the milk consumption for my family. _____

15. I have tried non-instant powdered milk from the natural food store. _____

16. I have tried vegetable juices. _____

CHAPTER 12

VITAMINS AND MINERALS

VITAMINS

Probably the most misunderstood subject along the "health line" is vitamins. Here are just a few of the questions people ask and argue about.

1. What vitamins should I take and how many?
2. Aren't synthetic vitamins the same as natural ones?
3. Shouldn't I take some vitamins with certain other vitamins?
4. Which brand is the best?
5. How can I be sure my vitamins do not contain sugar?
6. Isn't it dangerous to mix so many vitamins at one time?
7. I have heard that I should take a lot of Vitamin C when I get sick, but isn't that dangerous?
8. My doctor thinks vitamins are a lot of bologna. Should I still take them without telling him?
9. Since I eat good food, do I really need to take vitamins?

The list of questions is endless when it comes to taking supplements. Even the experts disagree. Just about the time you think you have found the answer to the question, you will read another article on the opposite side of the fence. Just to give you an idea of how fathomless this subject is, *Prevention* Magazine had over 174 articles on vitamins in 1977.

Let's begin with the last question. So many people say that since their diets contain good, wholesome food, then why is there a need to supplement it with vitamins? According to Robert Rodale's *The Complete Book of Vitamins,* there are six basic reasons why people need vitamins and minerals.

REASONS FOR VITAMINS

1. Soil depletion due to modern methods of farming.
2. Increasing use on crops of incredibly toxic pesticides and herbicides.
3. Tendency to pick and ship fruits and vegetables green rather than ripe.
4. Processing and chemicalizing food.
5. Overuse of pure, Vitamin-free sugar for as much as one-fourth of our average calorie intake.

6. Chemical additives in food, which are worthless nutritionally, but take the place of highly nutritious elements.

VITAMIN A

U.S. Recommended Daily Allowance: 5,000 I.U.

Other Name: Anti-Infective or Anti-Ophthalmic Vitamin

Measurement: U.S.P. Units or I.U. (International Units)

Fat Soluble

Complementary Nutrients: B complex, choline, C,D,E,F, calcium, phosphorus, zinc

Sources: Green and yellow fruits and vegetables, milk and dairy products, eggs, fish liver oils, liver, apricots, carrots

Anti-Vitamins: Alcohol, coffee, cortisone, excessive iron, Vitamin D deficiency

Bodily Parts Affected: Bones, eyes, hair, skin, soft tissue, teeth

Bodily Functions Affected: Helps the body fight infections, especially of the respiratory tract. Helps maintain a healthy condition of the outer layers of many tissues and organs. Permits formation of visual purple in the eye, helping to prevent night blindness and poor eyesight. Promotes healthy skin. It is needed for pregnancy and nursing mothers. Helps in the growing process.

Deficiency Causes: Allergies, sinus trouble, fatigue, loss of smell, blemishes, rough dry skin, appetite loss, night blindness, soft tooth enamel, susceptibility to infections, itching and burning eyes, dry hair.

Helpful Information: Vitamin A has been used in the treatment of cancer because it can enhance the body's defenses. The Germans have been using large doses of Vitamin A in an emulsified form. This emulsified form bypasses the liver, thus enabling a person to consume huge quantities of Vitamin A, without doing damage to the body. Vitamin A can also be purchased in the form of Lemon Grass Oil, which is water soluble.

Average Dosage: 10,000 units daily

B COMPLEX
VITAMIN B₁

U.S. Recommended Daily Allowance: 1.5 mg.

Other Name: Thiamine, Thiamine Chloride, Thiamine HCI, Thiamine Monoitrate. Also known as the Anti-Neuritic or Anti-Beriberi Vitamin

Measurement: Milligrams

Water Soluble

Complementary Nutrients: B Complex, B₂, folic acid, niacin, C, E, manganese, sulphur

Sources: Brewer's yeast, brown rice, whole wheat, oatmeal, blackstrap molasses, fish, nuts, beans

Anti-Vitamins: Alcohol, coffee, fever, raw clams, sugar (excessive), stress, surgery, tobacco

Bodily Parts Affected: Brain, ears, eyes, hair, heart, nervous system

Bodily Functions Affected: Helps growth, appetite, digestion, carbohydrate metabolism, energy, nerve tissues, muscles and heart. Essential in growth learning capacity.

Deficiency Causes: Beriberi, fatigue, vague aches and pains, pains around heart, appetite loss, insomnia, noise sensitivity, digestive disturbances, nervous irritability, numbness of hands and feet, mental depression, and shortness of breath and constipation.

Average Dosage: Usually taken with other B vitamins anywhere from 10 mg. to 50 mg. daily.

VITAMIN B₂

U.S. Recommended Daily Allowances: 1.7 mg.

Other Name: Riboflavin or Vitamin G

Measurement: Milligrams

Water Soluble

Complementary Nutrients: B Complex, B₆, niacin, C, phosphorus

Sources: Nuts, whole grains, blackstrap molasses, cheese, salmon, yeast, liver, most B₁ sources

Anti-Vitamins: Alcohol, coffee, sugar (excessive), tobacco

Bodily Parts Affected: Eyes, hair, nails, skin, soft body tissue

Bodily Functions Affected: Metabolism of carbohydrate, fat, and protein, cell respiration, and improves antibody and red blood cell formation. Promotes healthy skin and mouth. Needed for iron absorption.

Deficiency Causes: Inflammation of the mouth, itching and burning eyes, red sore tongue, cataracts, cracking of the corner of the lips, bloodshot eyes, poor digestion, and dizziness.

Average Dosage: Usually taken with other B Vitamins anywhere from 10 mg. to 50 mg. daily.

VITAMIN B$_3$

U.S. Recommended Daily Allowance: 20 mg.

Other Name: Niacin, Niacinamide, Nicotinic Acid, Niacin Amide, Nicotinamide

Measurement: Milligrams

Water Soluble

Complementary Nutrients: B Complex, B$_1$, B$_2$, C, Phosphorus

Sources: Brewer's yeast, wheat germ, brown rice, fish, milk, liver, nuts, sunflower seeds, peanuts, green vegetables, whole wheat products and potatoes

Anti-Vitamins: Alcohol, antibiotics, coffee, corn, sugar, starches (excessive)

Bodily Parts Affected: Nerves, brain, skin, liver, soft tissue, tongue

Bodily Functions Affected: Essential for a good nervous system and circulation. Maintains proper carbohydrate and protein metabolism. Helps in normal functioning of the intestinal tract. Helps with migraine headaches and the skin.

Deficiency Causes: Depression, diarrhea, appetite loss, pellagra, nervousness, canker sores, mental disease, skin lesions. insomnia, halitosis, fatigue, irritability, chronic headaches, muscular weakness, and digestive disorders.

Helpful Information: Niacin has been successfully used in the treatment of Schizophrenia.

Average Dosage: Usually taken with other B vitamins anywhere from 10 mg. to 50 mg. daily.

VITAMIN B$_5$

U.S. Recommended Daily Allowance: 10 mg.

Other Name: Pantothenic Acid, Calcium Pantothenate

Measurement: Milligrams

Water Soluble

Complimentary Nutrients: B Complex, B$_6$, B$_{12}$, biotin, folic acid, C

Sources: Brewer's yeast, wheat germ, liver, salmon, bran peas, beans, peanuts, crude molasses, egg yolk, green vegetables, whole grain breads, and cereals.

Anti-Vitamins: Alcohol, coffee

Bodily Parts Affected: Digestive tract, skin, adrenal glands, nerves

Bodily Functions Affected: Helps in building body cells and maintaining normal skin, and central nervous system. Needed to make antibodies. Helps the adrenal glands in the production of cortisone and other hormones. Protects against stress and toxins. Prevents premature aging. It is also good for anti-radiation protection.

Deficiency Causes: Eczema, intestinal disorders, muscle cramps, mental depression, diarrhea, hypoglycemia, kidney trouble, respiratory infections, duodenal ulcers, loss of hair, premature aging, restlessness, fatigue, low blood pressure, asthma, dizzy spells, burning feet, and allergies.

Average Dosage: Usually taken with other B vitamins anywhere from 20 to 50 mg. daily. Used with Folic Acid.

VITAMIN B6

U.S. Recommended Daily Allowance: 2 mg.

Other Name: Pyridoxine Hydrochloride

Measurement: Milligrams

Water Soluble

Complementary Nutrients: B Complex, B1, B2, pantothenic acid, C, magnesium, potassium, linoleic acid, sodium

Sources: Bananas, blackstrap molasses, brewer's yeast, green leafy vegetables, meat, fish, organ meats, wheat germ, whole grains, egg yolk, cantaloupe, cabbage, milk, pecans. Raw foods contain more B6 than cooked foods.

Anti-Vitamins: Alcohol, birth control pills, coffee, radiation (exposure), tobacco

Bodily Parts Affected: Blood, muscles, nerves, skin

Bodily Functions Affected: Helps antibody formation and digestion and enzymes. Maintains sodium potassium balance for nerves and skin and prevents nausea. Essential for proper fat and protein utilization. Necessary in pregnancy and works toward keeping cholesterol down.

Deficiency Causes: Nervousness, loss of muscular control, acne, convulsions in babies, insomnia, anemia, depression, arthritis, hair loss, learning disabilities, dizziness, irritability, and weakness. Destroyed by heat.

Helpful Information: Studies have shown that Vitamin B_6 is very helpful for women and their monthly cycle. Discomfort can be reduced greatly with a continued use of Vitamin B_6. It also helps water from building up in the tissues causing swelling.

Average Dosage: Usually taken with other B vitamins anywhere from 10 mg. to 50 mg. daily. When taken in addition to B Complex, dosage is 100 mg. to 150 mg. depending upon your body and your doctor.

VITAMIN B_9

U.S. Recommended Daily Allowance: .4 mg.

Other Name: Folic Acid, Folacin, Pteroylglutamic acid, Folate

Measurement: Milligrams

Water Soluble

Complementary Nutrients: B Complex, B_{12}, Biotin, Pantothenic Acid, C

Sources: Deep green leafy vegetables, whole grains, liver, Brewer's yeast, lima beans, Irish potatoes, oysters, salmon, lettuce, mushrooms, nuts, and milk

Anti-Vitamins: Alcohol, coffee, stress, tobacco

Bodily Parts Affected: Liver, blood and glands.

Bodily Functions Affected: It is needed for the formation of red blood cells by its action on the bone marrow. It is essential to normal growth and protein metabolism. Helps in healing processes. Contributes to the development of antibodies. It is necessary for the health of skin and hair, especially prevents graying.

Deficiency Causes: Anemia, digestive disturbances, graying hair, growth problems, serious skin disorders, impaired circulation, fatigue, mental depression, reproductive disorders.

Average Dosage: .1 to .4 mg. is usual dosage. Potencies higher than 0.1 in one tablet are available by prescription only.

VITAMIN B₁₂

U.S. Recommended Daily Allowance: 6 mcg.

Other Name: Cobalamin, Cyanocobalamin, "Red Vitamin"

Measurement: Micrograms (1,000 micrograms is equal to 1.0 milligrams)

Water Soluble

Complementary Nutrients: B Complex, B₆, choline, inositol, C, potassium, sodium

Sources: Cheese (Roquefort), fish, milk, bananas, milk products, organ meats, comfrey leaves, liver, peanuts

Anti-Vitamins: Alcohol, coffee, laxatives, tobacco

Bodily Parts Affected: Blood, nerves

Bodily Functions Affected: Helps in the formation and revitalization of red blood cells, thus helping to prevent anemia. Promotes appetite and healthy nervous system. Helps in metabolism.

Deficiency Causes: General weakness, nervousness, pernicious anemia, walking and speaking difficulties, sore mouth and loss of mental energy. The mineral cobalt is essential for the body to utilize B₁₂.

Average Dosage: 10 mcg. to 50 mcg. daily.

VITAMIN B₁₃

U.S. Recommended Daily Allowance: None has been established

Other Name: Orotic Acid

Complementary Nutrients: B Complex

Sources: Whey portion of milk, especially in soured milk

Bodily Parts Affected: Cells, liver

Bodily Functions Affected: It is necessary for rebuilding of cells.

Deficiency Causes: Deficiencies are not known, but it is believed that they may lead to liver disorders and cell degeneration and premature aging; also overall degeneration as in multiple sclerosis.

Average Dosage: Unknown

VITAMIN Bx

U.S. Recommended Daily Allowance: None has been established

Other Name: Para-amino-benzoic Acid, PABA

Measurement: Milligrams

Water Soluble

Complementary Nutrients: B Complex, Folic Acid, C

Sources: Blackstrap molasses, brewer's yeast, whole grain products, milk, eggs, yogurt, wheat germ

Anti-Vitamins: Alcohol, coffee, sulfa drugs

Bodily Parts Affected: Skin, hair, gland, and intestines

Bodily Functions Affected: Essential in growth working with Folic Acid. Keeps hair from turning gray and helps blood cell formation. It is needed for healthy skin and helps with the pain of burns.

Deficiency Causes: Fatigue, headaches, constipation, anemia, eczema, depression, gray hair, digestive disorders, headaches, reproductive disorders and irritability.

Average Dosage: Any doses higher than 30 mg. per tablet are available by prescription only.

CHOLINE

U.S. Recommended Daily Allowance: None has been established

Other Name: Members of B Complex family, and one of the "Lipotropic Factors"

Measurement: Milligrams

Water Soluble

Complementary Nutrients: A, B Complex, B12, Folic Acid, Inositol, Linoleic Acid

Sources: Lecithin, brewer's yeast, wheat germ, egg yolk, fish, legumes, organ meats, green leafy vegetables

Anti-Vitamins: Alcohol, coffee, sugar (excessive)

Bodily Parts Affected: Liver, hair, thymus gland and kidneys

Bodily Functions Affected: Regulates function of liver and is necessary for normal fat metabolism. It minimizes excessive deposits of fat in liver. Helps the liver and gallbladder. It is needed for phospholipid in the blood. It can prevent gallstones from forming. It helps reduce high blood pressure.

Deficiency Causes: Heart trouble, impaired liver and kidney function, bleeding stomach ulcers, intolerance to fats, growth problems, high blood pressure, atherosclerosis, and hardening of arteries.

Average Dosage: It should always be taken with B complex vitamins. Dosage can be 10 to 50 mg. High doses from 500 to 1,000 mg. should be under doctor's care.

INOSITOL

U.S. Recommended Daily Allowance: None has been established

Other Name: A member of the B Complex family

Measurement: Milligrams

Water Soluble

Complementary Nutrients: B Complex, B12, Choline, Linoleic Acid

Sources: Brewer's yeast, blackstrap molasses, citrus fruits, wheat germ, lecithin, unprocessed whole grains, nuts, milk, liver and vegetables

Anti-Vitamins: Alcohol, coffee

Bodily Parts Affected: Heart, liver, muscles, brain, kidneys, and hair

Bodily Functions Affected: Can prevent thinning hair and baldness. Can help reduce blood cholesterol, and is helpful for a healthy heart muscle.

Deficiency Causes: High cholesterol, constipation, eczema, eye abnormalities, hair loss.

Average Dosage: In one tablespoon of yeast there are 40 milligrams of choline and inositol. Authorities recommend taking the same amount of choline and inositol. Inositol is found more freely in the human body than any other vitamin with the exception of niacin.

BIOTIN

U.S. Recommended Daily Allowance: .3 mg.

Other Name: Vitamin H

Measurement: Milligrams or Micrograms

Water Soluble

Complementary Nutrients: B Complex, B12, Folic Acid, Pantothenic Acid, C, Sulphur

Sources: Brewer's yeast, whole grains, soybeans, liver, unpolished rice, eggs, beans, and peanuts

Anti-Vitamins: Alcohol, coffee, raw egg white

Bodily Parts Affected: Skin, muscles, and hair

Bodily Functions Affected: Builds cell growth and helps break down fats and proteins. It is used in the utilization of Vitamin B and associated with healthy growth and hair. It helps prevent hair loss.

Deficiency Causes: Skin disorders, heart abnormalities, anemia, extreme fatigue, eczema, loss of appetite, mental depression, dandruff, confusion, hair loss, lung infections, drowsiness and hallucinations.

Helpful Information: Used as an antiseptic and in the treatment of Malaria.

Average Dosage: .05 mg. approximately or 150 to 300 micrograms

<h2 style="text-align:center">B₁₅</h2>

U.S. Recommended Daily Allowance: None has been established

Other Name: Pangamic Acid, Calcium Pangamate

Measurement: Milligrams

Sources: Nuts, brown rice, whole grains, and seeds

Bodily Parts Affected: Nerves, blood, cells, heart and glands

Bodily Functions Affected: Helpful in breaking down fats. Essential for sufficient oxygen supply to the tissues and cells. It can help in the treatment of angina and heart disease, impaired circulation, high blood cholesterol, and premature aging. It works on the nervous system and glands. It also can assist in the damage caused by carbon monoxide poisoning.

Deficiency Causes: Heart disease, diseases related to the nervous system and glands, and hypoxia (lack of oxygen supply to the cells.)

Helpful Information: Used in Russia and some other countries, but has not been widely used in the U.S. Was discovered by Dr. Ernest Krebs.

Average Dosage: When prescribed, it is usually 50 mg. in the morning and 50 mg. at night. It can be 150 mg. to 300 mg., depending upon the doctor's orders.

<h2 style="text-align:center">B₁₇</h2>

U.S. Recommended Daily Allowance: None has been established—the U.S. does not recognize B_{17} as an official vitamin, even though it is used the world over.

Other Name: Nitrilosides, Amygdalin, Laetrile (when the body breaks it down)

Measurement: Milligrams

Water Soluble

Complementary Nutrients: All vitamins

Sources: Seeds, beans and sprouts, chart to follow

Anti-Vitamins: Alcohol, stress, sugar

Bodily Parts Affected: Total body

Bodily Functions Affected: Essential for the body's resistance to cancer.

Deficiency Causes: Prolonged deficiencies may lead to diminished resistance to malignancies.

Helpful Information: Vitamin B_{17} is not accepted officially as a vitamin in the U.S. However, it has been widely used in the rest of the world for over 25 years. It was isolated and given its name in 1953 by Dr. Ernest Krebs.

Average Dosage: Usual dosage for cancer prevention is a diet without poisons and high in the fruits and vegetables containing nitrilosides and a few apricot pits daily.

Cancer patients take high doses of Amygdalin (crushed apricot pits or other sources) in injectable form. As the tumors shrink the dosage is decreased to tablets.

FOODS HIGH IN NITRILOSIDES OR B17

BEANS:

Broad Beans
Burma Beans
Chick Peas
Lentils (sprouted)
Lima Beans
Mung Beans (sprouted)
Rangoon
Scarlet Runner

BERRIES:

Almost all wild berries
Blackberry
Chokeberry
Christmas Berry
Cranberry
Elderberry
Raspberry
Strawberry

GRASSES:

Acacia
Alfalfa (sprouted)
Aquatic
Johnson Grass
Milk Weed
Sudan Grass
Tunus Grass
Velvet Grass
Wheat Grass
White Clover

GRAINS:

Barley
Brown Rice
Buckwheat Groats
Chia
Flax
Millet
Oat Groats
Rye
Vetch
Wheat Berries

KENNELS OR SEEDS:

Apple
Apricot
Cherry
Nectarine
Peach
Pear
Plum
Prune

NUTS:

Almonds
Macadamia

SEEDS:

Chia
Flax
Sesame

MISCELLANEOUS:

Bamboo Shoots
Fuschia Plants
Sorghum Plant
Wild Hydrangea
Yew Tree (Needles, fresh leaves)

VITAMIN C

U.S. Recommended Daily Allowance: 60 mg.

Other Name: Ascorbic Acid, Cavitamin Acid

Measurement: Milligrams and sometimes units (1 mg. equals 20 units)

Water Soluble

Complementary Nutrients: All vitamins and minerals, bioflavonoids, calcium, magnesium

Sources: Citrus fruits, rose hips, black currants, broccoli, raw green bell peppers, guavas, strawberries, turnip greens, raw potatoes, apples, tomatoes, persimmons, acerola cherries, and cabbage

Anti-Vitamins: Antibiotics, aspirin, cortisone, high fever, stress, and tobacco

Bodily Parts Affected: Adrenal glands, blood, capillary walls, connective tissue (skin, ligaments, bones), gums, heart, and teeth

Bodily Functions Affected: Aids bone and teeth formation. Necessary for the proper functioning of collagen (intercellular cement). Needed for good gums and teeth. Helps in red blood cell formation. It is good for resistance to infection and colds. Necessary for adrenal and thyroid glands. Promotes wound healing.

Deficiency Causes: Anemia, bleeding gums, capillary wall ruptures, easily bruised, tooth decay, soft gums, premature aging, low infection resistance, nose bleeds, poor digestion, thyroid insufficiency and scurvy.

Helpful Information: Vitamin C is an "all around" resistor to ill health and especially the common cold. It counteracts the effects of harmful drugs and gives protection against stress. It protects the body against toxic chemicals in our food, water and air. Vitamin C has even been used with success in rattlesnake bite. It can be used as an antibiotic. It is helpful in cancer treatment.

Average Dosage: 500 mg. to 1,000 mg. daily. It has been said that Vitamin C is non-toxic. When fighting infection, it is better to take the Vitamin C every hour. The usual dosage for hourly intervals is between 1,000 mg. to 2,000 mg. If the body is not fighting infection and too much Vitamin C is taken, the result may be diarrhea. Massive doses of Vitamin C by injection are helpful when other antibiotics have failed. A better form of Vitamin C is from Rose Hips with Bioflavonoids, Rutin, Hesperidin, and Buckwheat.

VITAMIN D

U.S. Recommended Daily Allowance: 400 I.U.

Other Name: Ergosterol, Viosterol, Calciferol, "Sunshine Vitamin"

Measurement: U.S.P. Units

Fat Soluble

Complementary Nutrients: A, choline, C, E, Calcium, Phosphorus

Sources: Sunshine, sprouted seeds, fish liver oils, milk, sunflower seeds, butter, egg yolks and mushrooms

Anti-Vitamins: Mineral oil

Bodily Parts Affected: Bones, heart, nerves, skin, teeth, thyroid gland

Bodily Functions Affected: Regulates the use of calcium and phosphorus in the body and is therefore necessary for the proper formation of teeth and bones. It is also important for the parathyroid glands which controls the calcium level in the blood. Essential in preventing pyorrhea, tooth decay and rickets.

Deficiency Causes: Burning sensation in the mouth and throat, diarrhea, insomnia, myopia, nervousness, poor metabolism, softening bones and teeth and rickets.

Average Dosage: 400 I.U. is average dosage. Can be toxic if taken in excessive doses, especially by infants.

VITAMIN E

U.S. Recommended Daily Allowance: 30 I.U.

Other Name: Tocopherol, D-alpha tocopherol, dl-tocopherol (synthetic) mixed tocopherol

Measurement: International Units, sometimes milligrams. 1 I.U. equals 1 mg.

Fat Soluble

Complementary Nutrients: A, B Complex, B_1, Inositol, C, F. Manganese, Selenium, Phosphorus

Sources: Dark green vegetables, eggs, liver, wheat germ, that is fresh (less than a week old), unrefined cold-pressed crude vegetable oils, soybean oil, raw or sprouted seeds, nuts and grains, especially whole wheat.

Anti-Vitamins: Birth control pills, chlorine or chlorinated water, inorganic iron, estrogen, mineral oil, rancid fat and oil

Bodily Parts Affected: Cells, glands (adrenal and thyroid), hair, mucous membranes, nerves, skin

Bodily Functions Affected: It is helpful in blood cholesterol reduction. Vitamin E assists sex hormones, unsaturated fatty acis and fat soluble vitamins from being blotted out by oxygen. It dilates blood vessels and helps circulation. It also gives protection to the lungs from pollutants in the air. It helps stop the aging process and is necessary for healthy reproductive organs. Vitamin E does help in emphysema, arthritis, asthma, burns, phlebitis, leg ulcers, and prevents scar tissue in burns and sores. It is a natural anti-coagulant.

Deficiency Causes: Strokes, heart disease, pulmonary embolism, enlarged prostate gland, miscarriages, muscular destruction, sterility, dry dull or falling hair, and increased fragility of red blood cells.

Helpful Information: Vitamin E has been used successfully in treating burns. It has also been used in place of hormones after hysterectomy operations. Latest information shows that Vitamin E is quite valuable in clearing acne because of its close relation to the adrenal glands. Do not take inorganic Iron with Vitamin E.

Average Dosage: Approximately 200 I.U. a day. Therapeutic doses range from 200 to 2,400 I.U. daily depending upon the condition. Those people with heart conditions or high blood pressure should check with their doctor for proper dosage.

VITAMIN F

U.S. Recommended Daily Allowance: None has been established

Other Name: Unsaturated Fatty Acids, Linoleic and Linolenic being the most important fatty acids.

Measurement: Milligrams

Complementary Nutrients: A, C, D, E, phosphorus

Sources: Unprocessed and unrefined vegetable oils, especially safflower, soybean, corn, flaxseed and sunflower.

Anti-Vitamins: Radiation, x-rays

Bodily Parts Affected: Blood vessels, heart, lungs, nerves, pituitary glands, skin

Bodily Functions Affected: Helps prevent hardening of the arteries. It normalizes blood pressure and helps to lower blood cholesterol, thus preventing heart disease. Vitamin F is important in growth. It is necessary to healthy skin and all mucuous membranes. It is essential for the adrenal glands. Vitamin F helps calcium and phosphorus be available to the cells.

Deficiency Causes: Acne, allergies, diarrhea, dry skin, dry brittle hair, eczema, gall stones, nail problems, underweight, varicose veins, retarded growth, impairment in reproductive functions, kidney disorders and prostate disorders.

Average Dosage: According to the Natural Research Council, 1% of the total calories should be unsaturated fatty acids.

VITAMIN G

Other Name: Combination of Riboflavon and Thiamine

Helpful Information: Can be used in place of Valium or for stress

VITAMIN H

Other Name: Biotin (see earlier Biotin heading)

VITAMIN K

U.S. Recommended Daily Allowance: None has been established

Other Name: Menadione

Measurement: Milligrams

Sources: Egg yolks, kelp, liver, alfalfa, soybean oil, green plants, and cow's milk. It is also made in the intestines by normal bacteria.

Bodily Parts Affected: Blood, liver, nerves

Bodily Functions Affected: Vitamin K is essential for blood to clot. It is important to liver function. It helps the nervous system.

Deficiency Causes: Hemorrhages such as nosebleeds, and bleeding ulcers. Lowered vitality and premature aging.

Average Dosage: None has been established.

VITAMIN P

U.S. Recommended Daily Allowance: None has been established

Other Name: Citrus bioflavonoids, Bioflavonoid complex, Citrin, Hesperidin, Quercitin, Rutin, Part of a Citamin C Complex

Measurement: Milligrams

Water Soluble

Complementary Nutrients: Vitamin C

Sources: Peels and pulp of citrus fruit, especially lemon, fresh fruits and vegetables, buckwheat, green peppers, grapes, apricots, strawberries, black currants, cherries, and prunes.

Anti-Vitamins: Antiobiotics, aspirin, cortisone, high fever, stress, and tobacco

Bodily Parts Affected: Blood, capillary walls, connective tissue

Bodily Functions Affected: It helps maintain the blood vessel wall. Vitamin P gives strength to the capillary walls and prevents hemorrhaging and acts as an anti-coagulant, thus it may prevent strokes. It is helpful in varicose veins, bleeding gums, hypertension, coronary thrombosis, respiratory infections, cirrhosis of the liver, hemorrhoids, eczema, psoriasis, arteriosclerosis, retinal hemorrhages, homorrhaging, and radiation sickness. It is also helpful in cold and flu prevention.

Deficiency Causes: It may cause the appearance of purplish or blue spots on the skin. Lack of Vitamin P causes capillary fragility.

Average Dosage: Therapeutic doses range from 50 to 200 mg. or more. The FDA says that bioflavonoids do not have any value, either nutritionally or therapeutic.

VITAMIN T

U.S. Recommended Daily Allowance: None has been established

Other Name: Sesame Seed Factor

Sources: "Tahini," (raw sesame butter), sesame seeds, egg yolks and some vegetable oils.

Bodily Parts Affected: Blood

Bodily Functions Affected: Can be helpful in anemia. Helps the formation of blood platelets. Also good in improving fading memory.

Average Dosage: Unknown

VITAMIN U

U.S. Recommended Daily Allowance: None has been established

Sources: Raw cabbage juice, fresh cabbage, homemade sauerkraut

Bodily Parts Affected: Stomach, small intestines

Bodily Functions Affected: Vitamin U is a vitimin-like factor found in some vegetables, particularly cabbage. It helps promote healing in peptic ulcers, and especially in duodenal ulcers.

Average Dosage: Unknown

MINERALS

Minerals sometimes get lost in the shuffle behind vitamins, and yet, they are very important. Some authorities feel that lack of minerals can lead to cancer. Studies have shown that minerals are necessary nutrients to keep the body in tip-top shape. Even some deaths have been attributed to a deficiency in minerals. However, caution is given in regard to taking minerals as well as vitamins—consult your doctor. Any amount above the recommended daily allowance could be dangerous for your body.

CALCIUM

U.S. Recommended Daily Allowance: 800 mg. or 1.0 grams daily. Children need more.

Abbreviation: Ca

Sources: Milk, cheese, sesame seeds, green leafy vegetables.

Bodily Functions Affected: Builds and strengthens bones and teeth. It is essential for blood to clot. Calcium helps regulate the heart rhythm. It is used by the body with vitamins A, C, and D, and phosphorus.

Deficiency Causes: All bone related diseases, nervous disorders, muscle cramps, sleeplessness, rickets and depression.

CHLORINE

U.S. Recommended Daily Allowance: 500 mg.

Abbreviation: CL

Sources: Watercress, seaweed, cabbage, tomatoes, salt water fish, celery, pineapple and cucumber

Bodily Functions Affected: It is needed in producing hydrochloric acid in the stomach. Chlorine helps the liver and keeps the fluid level up in the body.

Deficiency Causes: Improper digestion and body fluid levels

CHROMIUM

U.S. Recommended Daily Allowance: None has been established.

Abbreviation: Cr

Sources: Hard water, brewer's yeast, whole grains, mushrooms

Bodily Functions Affected: It is necessary in maintaining correct cholesterol levels. Helps in the absorption of glucose from the blood. Involved with the heart.

Deficiency Causes: Hypoglycemia, diabetes, and heart disease.

COBALT

U.S. Recommended Daily Allowance: None has been established

Abbreviation: Co

Sources: Green leafy vegetables and liver

Bodily Functions Affected: Essential for the body to utilize vitamin B_{12}. It also helps in forming red blood cells. Vitamin B_{12} is needed for normal growth.

Deficiency Causes: Pernicious anemia

COPPER

U.S. Recommended Daily Allowance: 2 mg.

Abbreviation: Cu

Sources: Liver, beans, green leafy vegetables, almonds, raisins, any iron-rich foods.

Bodily Functions Affected: Needed for the absorption of iron. Helps form red blood cells and keeps hair color.

Deficiency Causes: Loss and graying of hair, anemia, and heart damage.

FLUORINE

U.S. Recommended Daily Allowance: None has been established

Abbreviation: F

Sources: Milk, cheese, steel cut oats, carrots, garlic and beet tops.

Bodily Functions Affected: Necessary for proper bones and teeth

Deficiency Causes: Too much sodium fluoride which is in fluoridated water is dangerous.

IODINE

U.S. Recommended Daily Allowance: .15 mg. or 150 micrograms

Abbreviation: I

Sources: Seaweed, kelp, dulse, seafood, fish liver oils, pineapples, turnip greens and garlic.

Bodily Functions Affected: It is needed for proper function of the thyroid gland. Helps the energy level and metabolism.

Deficiency Causes: May cause obesity, goiters, anemia, and tiredness.

IRON

U.S. Recommended Daily Allowance: 10 mg.-males, 18 mg.-females daily

Abbreviation: FE

Sources: Black molasses, brewer's yeast, bananas, apricots, whole grains, spinach, liver, egg yolks, peaches, and raisins

Bodily Functions Affected: Necessary for forming red blood cells and carrying oxygen in the blood.

Deficiency Causes: Low resistance to diseases, headaches, anemia, fatigue.

LITHIUM

U.S. Recommended Daily Allowance: None has been established

Abbreviation: Li

Source: Kelp

Bodily Functions Affected: Helps regulate the sodium level in the body. Necessary for the nervous system.

Deficiency Causes: Mental and nervous conditions. It can be toxic.

MAGNESIUM

U.S. Recommended Daily Allowance: 350-400 mg.

Abbreviation: Mg

Sources: Soybeans, beet tops, celery, endive, brown rice, sunflower and sesame seeds, nuts, alfalfa, apples, lemons, and whole grains.

Bodily Functions Affected: Essential for Calcium metabolism. Can help calm down a person. Necessary for proper nerves and muscles. Helpful in heart regulation and cholesterol.

MANGANESE

U.S. Recommended Daily Allowance: None has been established

Abbreviation: Mn

Sources: Spinach, Brussels sprouts, green leafy vegetables, raw egg yolk, kelp, peas, blueberries, oranges, grapefruit, apricots, and the outer covering of grains and nuts.

Bodily Functions Affected: Necessary for proper function of several enzymes. It is helpful in the action between the brain and nerves. Necessary in reproduction.

Deficiency Causes: Stunted growth, sterility, bone deficiencies and asthma.

MOLYBDENUM

U.S. Recommended Daily Allowance: None has been established

Abbreviation: Mo

Sources: Millet, buckwheat, brown rice, brewer's yeast, and beans

Bodily Functions Affected: Needed in carbohydrate metabolism and enzyme functioning. Helpful in copper poinsoning.

Deficiency Causes: Not known

PHOSPHORUS

U.S. Recommended Daily Allowance: 800 mg. or 1.0 gram—adults, 1,000 mg.—children

Abbreviation: P

Sources: Most vegetables, beans, dairy products, fish, seeds, grains, and dried fruits

Bodily Functions Affected: It is necessary for the utilization of calcium and Vitamin D. Essential for healthy teeth and bones. Important element in good brain function.

Deficiency Causes: Stunted growth, weakness, poor nerves and mental conditions

POTASSIUM

U.S. Recommended Daily Allowance: 2,000 mg.

Abbreviation: K

Sources: Sunflower seeds, potatoes, bananas, green leafy vegetables, milk, grains, and oranges.

Bodily Functions Affected: It is needed in heart action, muscles, nerves and enzymes. It is related to keeping the proper acid-alkaline balance. It is related to hormone production.

Deficiency Causes: Overload of sodium in the body. High blood pressure, hypoglycemia, and heart problems.

SELENIUM

U.S. Recommended Daily Allowance: None has been established

Abbreeviation: Se

Sources: Kelp, seafoods, brewer's yeast, milk, and many vegetables

Bodily Functions Affected: It is helpful in detoxifying the body from harmful poisons.

Deficiency Causes: Dysfunctioning of the body, especially the liver

SILICON

U.S. Recommended Daily Allowance: None has been established

Abbreviation: Si

Sources: Alfalfa, apples, grapes, almonds, sunflower seeds, onions, strawberries and beets

Bodily Functions Affected: Needed for normal growth and helpful in the body healing itself.

Deficiency Causes: Sleeplessness, poor hair and nails, deficient bone formation

SODIUM

U.S. Recommended Daily Allowance: 2 to 4 grams daily (Diets are usually sufficient in salt)

Abbreviation: Na

Sources: Watermelon, kelp, sea salt, celery, asparagus, romaine lettuce

Bodily Functions Affected: Necessary to keep the proper body fluid level. It is interrelated with potassium and chlorine, involving many body functions.

Deficiency Causes: Weakness, breathing difficulty, nausea, and muscle aches. Usually there is too much salt in the body rather than too little.

SULPHUR

U.S. Recommended Daily Allowance: None has been established

Abbreviation: S

Sources: String beans, soybeans, fish, radishes, turnips, onions, celery

Bodily Functions Affected: Necessary for good healthy skin, nails and hair.

Deficiency Causes: Hair, nail and skin problems.

ZINC

U.S. Recommended Daily Allowance: 15 mg.

Abbreviation: Zn

Sources: Sunflower seeds, bran, pumpkin seeds, brewer's yeast, onions, eggs, green leafy vegetables, sprouted seeds and grains, and milk

Bodily Functions Affected: Helpful in normal tissue functioning and protein and carbohydrate metabolism. Needed in the formation of sex organs. Helps in healing.

Deficiency Causes: Dysfunction of the reproductive organs, memory failure, hair problems and skin diseases

SUMMARY ON VITAMINS AND MINERALS

After reading about vitamins and minerals, one can see the problems involved in giving simple answers to the questions given at the beginning of the chapter. Many people will give you many different answers. The best answer is to study your own body, check with a good nutritional doctor, and have him tell you what is best for you. Self diagnosis can be dangerous at times. However, you can help your doctor by reading informative articles and studying your own body peculiarities.

If you decide to take vitamins, then it would be good to start with a multi-vitamin. Ask for the best brand at a natural food store and compare the label with inferior brands. In this way you can see how much more you are getting for your money. Travel from store to store seeking the knowledge of others. Or use the multi-vitamin recommended by your doctor.

What about synthetic vitamins? Chemists will argue that all vitamins are the same within the body, however some experts feel that the body does indeed know the difference. I have personally seen where synthetic vitamins caused certain reactions and then natural vitamins were taken without the previous reaction. If a source is not given on the label, chances are it is synthetic. Most natural vitamins are from vegetables, grains, fruits or fish oils. Synthetic vitamins are usually from acids, chlorides, and chemicals. Vitamin E can either be from mixed tocopherols (several sources) or tocopherol acetate concentrate (one source). Natural is denoted by d-alpha and synthetic is dl-alpha. Read the label to know what you are getting.

Vitamins should be taken during the day and at mealtime so that they can work together. All the B Complex vitamins should be used as a group. Inorganic iron works against Vitamin E. Vitamins and minerals can be taken throughout the day instead of all at once. High doses of vitamins or minerals for extended periods of time can be dangerous and one should always check with a doctor before starting treatment. Since Vitamin C goes through the body, it is best to take it throughout the day when ill. Your body will develop diarrhea if too much Vitamin C is taken. Studies have shown that injectable Vitamin C was helpful in severe illnesses.

Some brands of vitamins are better than others because of containing no sugar, no preservatives, no coloring and no synthetic ingredients. There will always be the top of the line in any field. Many factors enter the picture such as cost, availability, and the importance of the vitamin. If you have a definite need for a certain vitamin, then perhaps you should spend the extra to have the best. Minerals are very important to our bodies. and often neglected. Reading the labels will help one to become familiar with the ingredients. The words, "chelated," "gluconate," and "orotate," appear on some vitamins and minerals. Each refers to a process which helps the body to assimilate the vitamins and minerals better. Those labeled "orotate" are the easiest for the body to utilize.

If your doctor feels that vitamins are unnecessary, perhaps you could help him by giving him informative articles on health and nutrition. Most doctors receive very little nutritional training in college. In fact, the average time spent on the subject is about two hours and only 19 out of 122 medical schools include nutritional courses. Many doctors are now beginning to see the correlation between diet and disease. Be a friend to your doctor and try to help him, if he lacks knowledge in this area.

People on a cancer control program should be taking all vitamins and minerals with emphasis on Vitamins A and C.

You be the judge and decide for yourself on the vitamin question.

CHAPTER 13

WHAT DOTH IT PROFIT A MAN?

WHAT DOTH IT PROFIT A MAN?

Now that you have learned many ways to help your body, you must consider this question. "For what is a man profited, if he shall gain the whole world, and lose his own soul?" Matthew 16:26. I like to paraphrase it to say,

What does it profit a man to gain all this knowledge about a healthy body, and yet lose his own soul for all eternity?

That would be very foolish, now wouldn't it? If a person is smart enough to realize that the right kind of food can help his body function better, then certainly he will be smart enough to know that his soul is eternal. This brings us to a question that only you can answer. Where will your soul be for all of eternity? This question is more important than the entire book you have just read.

ETERNITY IS FOREVER

"Eternal existence of the soul" is written upon the heart of every man. God put it there and we know it! Whether or not we believe it, is another problem. And since we are a free agent, God gives us a choice. We can actually choose our eternal destiny. Many people feel that this subject is not important and therefore they will postpone making a decision. In all reality, these people have made their decision, and it is no. God is not in the "middle-of-the-road" business. He is almighty and just and He doesn't change from year to year like the fashions. His Eternal Offer was made years ago and it still holds true today.

"But he was wounded for our transgressions, he was bruised for our iniquities: the chastisement of our peace was upon him; and with his stripes we are healed.

All we like sheep have gone astray; we have turned every one to his own way; and the Lord hath laid on him the iniquity of us all."

Isaiah 53:5-6

This Scripture was written by Isaiah many years before the Lord Jesus Christ was born, and yet, he describes perfectly the condition we are all in and what the Savior did on the cross.

WHO IS JESUS CHRIST?

He is Lord. He is called Wonderful, Counsellor, The mighty God, The everlasting Father, The Prince of Peace. He is the Alpha and Omega, or beginning and end. He is the Life, the Lamb, and the Light of the world. He is Lord of lords. He is the Jehovah of the Old Testament and the Messiah of the New Testament. He is the Rose of Sharon and the Bright and Morning Star. He is the Shepherd and Savior. He is the Redeemer, the Resurrection, and the Rock of all ages. He is the Way, the Truth, and the Life. He is truly the Son of God.

Perhaps you know or have heard all about the Lord Jesus. But maybe you have never realized exactly what He did for you. He left the beautiful splendor of heaven and humbled Himself to become a man here on earth. Then He fulfilled the Scriptures that had been written many years before and went to the cross to die a horrible death that you and I might have eternal life. But he didn't stay in the tomb, but was resurrected and now is in heaven.

WHY DID THE LORD JESUS PAY FOR MY SIN?

Why was it necessary for the only begotten Son of God to die on the cross and shed His precious blood for the sin of mankind. Yes, God made this provision after Adam and Eve had sinned in the Garden of Eden. The entire Old Testament tells of the coming of Christ. Since sin is not allowed in Heaven, God provided His Son, the Lord Jesus to become sin for us, that you and I might enter Heaven some day. Isn't it wonderful to realize that God cared enough about each one of us to allow the Lord Jesus to be payment for our sins. John 3:16 says it beautifully:

"For God so loved the world, that he gave his only begotten Son, that whosoever believeth in him should not perish, but have everlasting life."

It's God's love toward us that permitted the Lord Jesus to die in our place. Actually, when you get right down to it, all of us have sinned. The Bible clearly says that "There is none righteous, no not one." Everyone of us deserve punishment for our sin, but God is a loving and just God. He gave us a Gift.

THE GIFT TO THE WORLD

Let's suppose it is Christmas time and one of your friends gives you a lovely present. The gift is handed to you and you open it. You did not work for this gift nor did you give your friend any money to buy it. It was a gift out of love. Your friend paid the price for it. Your friend bought it with hard earned money.

This illustrates how the Lord Jesus is the Gift to the World. You can't pay for the work He did on Calvary. You can't earn your way to heaven. You can't give your money to someone else and let him work to heaven for you. You can't try to be "good" all your life and expect good works to get you to heaven. The Bible tells us "All of our righteousness is as filthy rags." If we worked for something, it certainly wouldn't be a gift. The Scripture tells us that Jesus is the Gift:

"For the wages of sin is death; but the gift of God is eternal life through Jesus Christ our Lord." Romans 6:23

And the Scripture that tells us we can't work to get to heaven is Ephesians 2:8 and 9:

"For by grace are ye saved through faith; and that not of yourselves; it is the gift of God; Not of works, lest any man should boast."

The Lord made salvation free to us because He knew some of us would never be rich enough to purchase eternal life and He knew we would never be perfect.

Isn't it a comforting fact to know that Jesus is a Gift to us and we don't have to pay or work to have this Gift.

THE UNOPENED GIFT

But let's carry our Christmas illustration one step further. Remember the friend, who brought you a gift? Let's say the friend brought the gift to your house and then left. You sat and looked at the gift, but did not open it. As a matter of fact, even after Christmas you still had not opened your friend's gift. There the gift sat all year long—unopened and even getting dusty. I know your friend would be hurt that you did not acknowledge the gift. You knew the gift was there, but you had never really received it.

This is exactly what so many people do with the Lord Jesus. They know He is the Gift to the world. They know that He died for their sins. They know that He paid their penalty on the cross so that they might have eternal life. And yet, the Gift is unopened. They have never received the Lord Jesus Christ as their own personal Gift. To these people, He is like the unopened Christmas Gift.

WILL YOU RECEIVE THE GIFT?

Perhaps you are one of these people who have always postponed receiving the Gift of the World, the Lord Jesus Christ. Now that you are interested in helping your body, why not make sure that your soul will have eternal life with its Maker? God, Himself, will give you the power to become His child. Are you willing to open the Gift?

"But as many as received him, to them gave he power to become the sons of God, even to them that believe on his name;" John 1:12

The Bible is clear on what we must do:

"That if thou shalt confess with thy mouth the Lord Jesus, and shalt believe in thine heart that God hath raised him from the dead, thou shalt be saved. For with the heart man believeth unto righteousness and with the mouth confession is made unto salvation." Romans 10:9, 10

No one can make this important decision for you. God knows your heart and He knows if you truly mean what you say. He knows if you have been "faking" it for all these years. If you would like to open the Gift and receive the Lord Jesus Christ as your Personal Savior, then pray this simple prayer right now.

Dear Lord Jesus, I admit I am a sinner and I'm sorry. Please forgive me of all my sin. Come into my heart and save me, making me a child of God. Thank you Lord Jesus for dying on the cross and saving me. Amen.

NOW THAT YOU'RE BORN AGAIN

If you were sincere when you prayed and asked Christ to come into your heart you became a child of God. This is being born again. At this moment you were spiritually baptised into the family of God. (I Corianthians 12:13). Now God's Spirit lives in you and bears witness with your spirit that you may know you are a child of God and should live for Him. (Romans 8:16).

What happens the next time you do something wrong? After all no one is perfect, we learned that earlier. Does this mean that a person must receive Christ all over again. No, I John 1:9 tells us what we must do:

"If we confess our sins, he is faithful and just to forgive us our sins, and to cleanse us from all unrighteousness."

Since our sin has been forgiven, then we must tell the Lord we are sorry for "slipping up" and the fellowship is restored. Here are a few ways that you can learn to grow as a Christian:

1. Read your Bible daily
2. Pray to the Lord daily
3. Tell others that you are saved
4. Confess your sins immediately
5. Serve the Lord in a Bible believing, fundamental church where the people are carrying their Bibles to church.
6. Be baptised by water according to the scriptures.
7. Live for the Lord daily.

If you prayed that prayer and are now born again, why not write to me?

Diane Campbell
c/o C C Publishers
P.O. Box 4044
Clearwater, Florida 33518

STEP-BY-STEP CHECK LIST TO NATURAL FOOD

If you have answered "yes" to every question on the STEP-BY-STEP CHECK LISTS for the entire book, then give yourself credit for doing a job well done. I know it may have been very difficult at times, but perseverance always pays off. Congratulations for "sticking" with it. I know you won't be sorry and your family will some day thank you. Of course, you must realize that a year or two of eating properly cannot eliminate twenty or forty years of body abuse. Sometimes it takes years to correct a problem or control a disease.

Since you have come this far with natural food, my prayer is that you will continue.

If you need any help locating health minded organizations, write to me in care of the publisher.

ACKNOWLEDGEMENTS

The following people were helpful in getting this book ready for publication. Many of them donated recipes. Some of the recipes were used as stepping stones to other recipes. Other people on this list gave me articles of interest, looked up information, or did other favors. I thank all of them for their help and continued interest in Natural Foods.

Barbara Banis
Dana Briggs
Gladys Bruce
Helen Campbell
Cindy Cummings
Norene Dobbs
Cheryl Doyle
Myrteen George
Karen Hone
Norman and Mary Hughes
Yvonne Johnson
Dian Johnson

William & Marzanna Krupp
Janet La Rue
Anna Michael
Rosalind Moore
Paulette Parker
Diana Rassi
Fran Rassi
Terry Riedel
Jackie Rupp
Mary Sandifer
Doris Walters
Ida Witt
Nina Zeidman

Extra thanks goes to Rosalind Moore for proofreading, creating and testing recipes, Barbara Banis for testing bread recipes and typing, Dr. Hazel Craig for proofreading, and Margaret Shettel for typing. Special thanks to Mary and Ken Sandifer for the creative art and photography. We appreciate the use of Mr. and Mrs. Waldense Malouf's home and staircase. We thank Betty Brewer and Dave Moriarity for typesetting, Great Outdoors Publishing Company for printing, Valkyrie Press, and Dr. Byron Goldberg.

BIBLIOGRAPHY

Abrahamson, E. M., and Pezet, A. W. *Body, Mind, and Sugar*, New York: Pyramid, 1971.

Airola, Dr. Paavo. *How To Get Well*, Phoenix, Arizona: Health Plus Publishers, 1974.

Atkins, Robert C., M. D. and Shirley Linde. *Dr. Atkins' Super-Engery Diet*, New York, New York: Bantam Books, Inc., 1978.

Betty Crocker's Cookbook, New York: Golden Press, 1972.

Campbell, Diane. *Naturally Good Cookbook*, Clearwater, Florida: 1977.

Clark, Linda. *Know Your Nutrition*, New Canaan, Connecticut: Keats Publishing, Inc., 1973.

Collier's Encyclopedia, New York, New York: P. F. Collier & Son Corporation, 1957, Volumes 1-20.

Cooking for Two, U.S. Department of Agriculture, Program #8, 1043, Food & Nutrition Service.

Davis, Adelle. *Let's Cook It Right*, New York, New York: The New American Library, 1970.

Dufty, William. *Sugar Blues*, New York, New York: Warner Books, 1975.

Dworkin, Stan and Floss. *Blend it Splendid*, Emmaus, Pennsylvania: Rodale Press, Inc., 1973.

Dworkin, Stan and Floss. *The Good Goodies*, Emmaus, Pennsylvania: Rodale Press, Inc., 1976.

Encyclopedic Cookbook, Chicago, Illinois: Book Production Industries, Inc., 1964.

Ford, Frank. *The Simpler Life Cookbook from Arrowhead Mills*, Ft. Worth, Texas: Harvest Press, 1974.

Fredericks, Carlton, and Herman Goodman. *Low Blood Sugar and You*, New York: Constellation International, 1969.

Griffin, G. Edward. *World Without Cancer*, Part I and Part II, Westlake, California: American Media, 1974.

Honey Recipe Book, Marketing Division, Iowa Department of Agriculture, 1971.

Hunter, Beatrice Trum. *The Natural Food Cookbook*, New York, New York: Pyramid Communications, Inc., 1975.

Hunsberger, Eydie Mae. *How I Conquered Cancer Naturally* Irvine, California: Harvest House Publishers, 1975.

Illustrated Davis Dictionary of the Bible, Nashville, Tennessee: Royal Publishers, Inc., 1973.

Ironside, H. A. *Daniel*, Neptune, New Jersey: Loizeaux Brothers, 1920.

Joseph, Jack. "Sugar is Sweet and Dangerous," *Bestways*, April, 1976.

Keil, C. F. and Delitzsch, F. *Biblical Commentary on the Old Testament*, Grand Rapids: Wm. B. Eerdmans Publishing Co., 1968, Daniel.

Kirban, Salem. *Health Guide to Survival*, Huntington Valley, Pennsylvania: Salem Kirban, Inc., 1976.

Kirschner, H. E. *Live Food Juices*, Monrovia, California: 1960.

Lappe, Frances Moore. *Diet for a Small Planet*, New York, New York: Ballentine Books, 1975.

McKibbin, Frank and Jean. *Cookbook of Foods from Bible Days*, Northridge, California: Voice Publications, 1971.

Naturally Great Foods, Emmaus, Pennsylvania: Rodale Press Inc., 1978.

Nave, Orville J. *Nave's Topical Bible*, Nashville, Tennessee:
The Southwestern Co., 1962.

Newman, J. M. *The Quest for Health,* Coalmont, Tennessee:
Journal of Natural Living.

Nittler, Dr. Alan H. *New Breed of Doctor*, New York:
Pyramid Books, 1972.

Oden, Rev. Clifford. *Thank God I Have Cancer!* Los Altos,
California: Freedom of Choice Publishers, Inc., 1976.

Patrick, Jay. "A Nation of Addicts," *Let's Live*, June, 1976.

Prevention Magazine. Emmaus, Pennsylvania: Rodale Press, Inc.,
1975, 1977, and 1978.

Reuben, Dr. David. *The Save Your Life Diet*, New York:
Ballantine Books, 1976.

Reuben, Dr. David and Barbara. *The Save-Your-Life-Diet High-Fiber
Cookbook*, New York: Ballantine Books, 1977.

Rodale, Robert. *The Complete Book of Vitamins*, Emmaus,
Pennsylvania: Rodale Press, Inc., 1966

Rodale, Robert. *The Prevention System*, Emmaus,
Pennsylvania: Rodale Press, Inc., 1976.

Smith, Dr. Lendon H. *Improving Your Child's Behavior Chemistry*,
Englewood Cliffs, New Jersey: Prentice-Hall, Inc., 1976.

Strong, James. *Strong's Exhaustive Concordance of the Bible*,
New York: Abingdon Press, 1967.

The Holy Bible, King James Version.

Today's Living. New York, New York: Syndicate Magazines,
Inc., September, 1976, Volume 7, No. 9.

Unger, Merrill F. *Unger's Bible Dictionary*, Chicago, Illinois:
Moody Press, 1966.

Vincent, Marvin R. *Word Studies in The New Testament,* Grand Rapids, Michigan: Wm. B. Eerdmans Publishing Co., Volume I, 1965.

Wuest, Kenneth S. *Word Studies in the Greek New Testament,* Grand Rapids, Michigan: Wm. B. Eerdmans Publishing Co., 1966.

Young, Robert. *Young's Analytical Concordance to The Bible,* Grand Rapids, Michigan: Wm. B. Eerdmans Publishing Co.

Yudkin, Dr. John. *Sweet and Dangerous,* New York: Bantam Books, 1972.

INDEX

214

TO ORDER MORE COPIES

If you have friends who are interested in having a copy of STEP-BY-STEP TO NATURAL FOOD, just send the coupon below. Why not give one as a gift?

Clip and Mail

Please send me _____copy(ies) at $6.95 plus .50 shipping and handling per copy.

_____Enclosed is my check for $ _____

_____Send C.O.D.

(Please Print)

Name_____

Address _____

City _____State_____Zip_____
Send To;
CC Publishers
P.O. Box 4044
Clearwater, FL 33518